STORIES OF STUDENT TEACHING

A Case Approach to the Student Teaching Experience

Debra Eckerman Pitton

GUSTAVUS ADOLPHUS COLLEGE

Merrill,
an imprint of Prentice Hall
Upper Saddle River, New Jersey   Columbus, Ohio

Library of Congress Cataloging-in-Publication Data
Pitton, Debra Eckerman.
        Stories of student teaching : a case approach to the student teaching experience /
Debra Eckerman Pitton.
            p.   cm.
        Includes bibliographical references and index.
        ISBN 0-13-437310-3 (paper)
        1. Student teaching—United States—Case studies.   I. Title.
    LB2157.U5P58   1998
    370.'71—DC21   96-49892
                                                                                                          CIP

Cover art: Matthew Wawiorka/Stock Illustration Source
Editor: Debra A. Stollenwerk
Production Editor: Louise N. Sette
Copy Editor: Lucinda A. Peck
Design Coordinator: Julia Zonneveld Van Hook
Text Designer: STELLARViSIONs
Cover Designer: Proof Positive/Farrowlyn and Associates
Production Manager: Laura Messerly
Director of Marketing: Kevin Flanagan
Advertising/Marketing Coordinator: Julie Shough
Electronic Text Management: Marilyn Wilson Phelps, Matthew Williams, Karen L. Bretz,
    Tracey Ward

This book was set in Zapf Calligraphic 801 by Prentice Hall and was printed and bound by
Quebecor Printing/Book Press. The cover was printed by Phoenix Color Corp.

 © 1998 by Prentice-Hall, Inc.
Simon & Schuster/A Viacom Company
Upper Saddle River, New Jersey 07458

Printed in the United States of America

10 9 8 7 6 5 4 3 2 1

ISBN: 0-13-437310-3

Prentice-Hall International (UK) Limited, *London*
Prentice-Hall of Australia Pty. Limited, *Sydney*
Prentice-Hall of Canada, Inc., *Toronto*
Prentice-Hall Hispanoamericana, S. A., *Mexico*
Prentice-Hall of India Private Limited, *New Delhi*
Prentice-Hall of Japan, Inc., *Tokyo*
Simon & Schuster Asia Pte. Ltd., *Singapore*
Editora Prentice-Hall do Brasil, Ltda., *Rio de Janeiro*

This text is dedicated to the many student teachers with whom I have worked over the years. I appreciate their willingness to share their experiences with me—both the successes and the struggles. The dedication of these individuals and their efforts to continue to learn and grow as educators speaks well of the future of our schools.

In addition, I want to express my appreciation to my husband, Jon, and my children, Angela, Matthew, and Laura. Their support and cooperation during the writing of this book were important elements in my successful completion of these stories.

PREFACE

Stories of Student Teaching: A Case Approach to the Student Teaching Experience is a result of seven years of interaction with student teachers and teacher preparation programs. While working with student teachers, I often find that they are so focused on the day-to-day preparation and execution of their lessons that they are unable to step back and reflect about what is happening. Case studies provide an effective technique for engaging preservice teachers in thoughtful analysis and dialogue regarding situations they may encounter in their student teaching experience. As Schulman (1992) says, "Cases are occasions for offering theories to explain why certain actions are appropriate" (p. 3). The richness of the narratives in this text provides countless opportunities for novice teachers to make connections between what they have learned in their classes and the world of teaching. The use of cases provides a bridge from the theoretical to the practical.

RATIONALE

Dealing with problems in education is never easy. There are seldom clear-cut solutions. Many factors often influence and compound a situation, and there are always multiple perspectives of the problem. While pedagogy is the usual focus in teacher-training classrooms, the student teaching experience brings into play the emotional context of the school community. Preservice teachers need to be aware of the importance of the relationships that exist within the student teaching environment, as well as the stress that these interactions can produce (Pitton, 1994).

The cases that make up this text are a slice of reality that present the multilayered experiences of student teachers. Shor (1987) describes the Freirean approach to teaching where problems are posed and solved by students themselves. This method empowers learners to take charge of their own learning. Future teachers who address problems posed by their peers in these cases and who analyze these interactions are formulating options for dealing with these situations in their own future classrooms.

Reading the cases and discussing the questions presented in this book force prospective teachers to identify problems. Beginning teachers often do not look deeply enough into a situation and thus fail to see the underlying causes of many problems (Berlinger, 1991). By engaging in discussion using cases that focus on difficulties that can arise in student teaching, future educators are able to develop problem-solving strategies. In this way, they are better prepared to identify the source of the difficulty. According to Merseth (1992), "Teachers need analytic and decision-making skills to make thoughtful assessments that induce appropriate action. Decision-making cases can hone these skills" (p. 53). By analyzing the effectiveness of the choices made by the individuals involved in a case, preservice teachers can learn to draw on their knowledge and consider possible alternative methods of handling problems in the classroom.

Most veteran teachers have years of experiences and interactions that provide options for dealing with situations in the classroom. Novice educators do not have such a repertoire. Cases help future teachers analyze the complexities of classroom difficulties and provide a context for discussion that links theory with the reality of the classroom. A student-centered discussion allows preservice teachers an opportunity to deal with a situation as they would in real life. How would they handle themselves if they faced a similar problem? What ideas can their colleagues offer? Where can they go for additional resources? What information from their knowledge of pedagogy can they draw on to assist them in their decision? Cases allow students to reflect about what is happening in the classroom depicted in the case—a type of perceptive thinking that has been identified as an important component in effective teaching (Schon, 1987).

The key to effective use of this text rests on the instructor's role in presenting the cases. Serving as a guide or reference, the instructor can facilitate student reflection and problem solving by using these cases and allowing the future teacher to build up a mental file of methods for dealing with similar situations. Upon completion of this book, preservice teachers should be able to identify areas where they, too, might have difficulties and work to strengthen their knowledge and skills.

A KEY FOCUS—REALITY-BASED CASES

The individuals involved in the problems described in this text have faced a difficult situation and responded to the issues as best they could. While some collections of case studies provide only the problem and encourage readers to resolve the dilemma, this text is reality-based. In real life, people deal with problems as best they can. Including the outcomes for most of these cases enables students to analyze the results and determine if the action taken by the student teacher was indeed the best approach.

This text intends to convey that all problems can be handled and that positive outcomes can occur even when mistakes have been made. This is an important message to send to all future educators. Few student teachers and beginning teachers complete their initial classroom experiences without acknowledging that they could have done some things better. We can learn from the mistakes of others and, hopefully, from our own errors. The decisions made by the teachers in this text provide models on which novice teachers can continue to reflect and consider new possibilities for dealing with difficulties in their own work.

When working through problems they encounter as beginning educators, new teachers do not have their college professors around to give them feedback. You will find no concluding remarks or response from experts in this reality-based text. Teachers have to seek out colleagues and other resources to reaffirm the decisions they make. They must deal with situations as they occur, and rarely do they have time for lengthy research. Reading and responding to the cases in this book with other preservice teachers under the guidance of an instructor provides future teachers an opportunity to learn to draw on the knowledge gained in their preservice coursework, to reflect on the best course of action, to discuss the cases with colleagues, to seek additional information as needed, and to determine the appropriate response to the situation. They will need to engage in this reflective problem-solving procedure when they are student teaching, as well as throughout the rest of their teaching career. This text provides an opportunity for student teachers to rehearse in a safe environment what they are expected to put into practice.

ORGANIZATION

Part One of these cases, "Eyewitness Accounts," contains the reflections of student teachers as they think back to their experiences in the classroom. Part Two, "Twice-Told Tales," identifies situations from the perspective of a supervisor who worked with the student teacher. Part Three, "Looking Back," gives us a more holistic perspective of student teaching and points out the drawbacks, as well as the learning opportunities, that can be a part of the student teaching experience.

TOPICS

The table of contents identifies the grade level and major issue contained in each case. However, these are multilayered cases that reflect the dynamic aspect of classroom life, and thus many problems are often embedded in each story. Lesson planning, classroom management, selection of curriculum and method of teaching, as well as assessment, inclusion, and parent interactions are key areas addressed in this text. In addition, the inter- and intrapersonal aspects of the student teaching experience are presented. This focus on the human element, the emphasis on the relationships that are integral to successful student teaching, is an important element of this book.

SUPPORTING FEATURES

The following introduction and teacher notes provide information for the instructor in the areas of case methodology and offer suggestions for using this text in the classroom. All cases are prefaced with questions to focus readers' thoughts and generate personal connections prior to reading. Follow-up questions are provided to extend the thinking and create connections for students between their coursework and the case. In addition, suggested readings have been identified so that students can extend their learning by investigating other sources.

CASES AND THE STUDENT TEACHING EXPERIENCE

The student teaching experience is a unique time. It is the moment future teachers are poised on the brink of their careers. Having completed the required coursework and initial clinical experiences, new teachers are now ready to practice their craft in a long-term, real-world situation. They move into a classroom that is the responsibility of another educator—someone they may or may not know well and with whom they may or may not share a common educational philosophy. Under the watchful eye of these experienced teachers, and with the guidance of college supervisors, novice educators enter this apprenticeship and practice their craft.

While some may question the validity of this current model, it is clear that a successful student teaching experience is vital for all individuals hoping for careers in education. A key factor in this situation, and one that compounds the stress felt by many student teachers, is the fear of the unknown. Most student teachers are not familiar with the school environment, the classroom, or the educator with whom they will be working. They lack experience in the day-to-day reality of the classroom and are often nervous about the situations they encounter and the types of problems that may arise during student teaching. Future educators do not want to appear unskilled or inept, so sharing their personal fears or problems in classes or seminars may often be too great a risk for them to take. Competition for future jobs and a desire to "look good" often inhibit the very conversations that might enable student teachers to learn and grow by analyzing their mistakes.

While the intent of student teaching is to provide preservice teachers opportunities to fine-tune their skills in a supportive environment, the very nature of the experience is fraught with stress. Even in the best placements, student teachers often feel enormous pressure: Will they succeed? Will they get a good recommendation (the key to securing a job)? What does their cooperating teacher really want of them? Is the college supervisor pleased with their development? Are they really doing a good job? Are the children learning?

No matter how comfortable the relationship is between individuals involved in this experience, student teachers will leave these situations with an evaluation that comments on their level of success. Because many student teaching situations are still only one semester in length, enormous pressure is put on novice teachers to make major strides in development in a relatively short time. Few student teachers want to acknowledge that they may be judged on their ability to head off problems or deal effectively with difficulties when they occur. A common complaint by student teachers is that, while they really just wanted to teach, they weren't given the opportunity because they were so busy dealing with problems in the classroom.

Handling the multidimensional issues that are a part of teaching in today's world is a complex task. What will be expected of new teachers when they are hired for their first classroom positions? How can student teachers develop the ability to problem-solve and the capability to be flexible so they can continue to learn and grow as educators? What level of development should novice teachers acquire during student teaching? These questions should be addressed prior to student teaching or at seminar sessions during the student teaching experience so that novice teachers are aware of the expectations for their performance during student teaching.

Many teacher preparation programs now include requirements for classroom involvement prior to student teaching to facilitate discussions of teaching situations. However, many of these programs are short-term connections that do not provide the time for students to experience the full range of issues that reflect the complexities of teaching. Opportunities to extend learning beyond these practicum experiences are needed. This book provides a realistic look into the student teaching experience for preservice teachers who will soon be heading out to their placements, as well as for individuals currently engaged in their student teaching experience. Written about actual situations from the vantage point of the student teacher or college supervisor who was involved, these narratives present multilevel problems and situations that occur in classrooms where student teachers work. The difficulties described in this text provide a safe vehicle for discussing problems for those who hesitate to reveal their own concerns. Novice teachers can analyze the situations, discuss their views with their peers and professors, and apply the analysis and new ideas to their own experience.

By addressing the situations provided in this book, preservice teachers can see that they are not alone in their fears, that what they may be experiencing is common for teachers in the early stages of their development. This book is written from the following perspective: that developing a spirit of comradery, sharing stories, and learning from other beginners' experience is necessary for the development of a competent educator and vital for the completion of a successful student teaching experience.

TEACHER NOTES

The cases in this text may be used in a variety of ways. Students can be encouraged to read on their own and reflect on the questions prior to attending class. The cases can be the basis for an entire preservice course or student teaching seminar sessions, or they can be layered into the curricula of existing classes. Interdisciplinary groups can be assigned specific cases to read and then present their collective thoughts to the whole group. These cases may also be used to facilitate a whole-class discussion, or students can write in their journals about any parallels to their own experience. Students who are currently engaged in student teaching may find these cases to be a safe way to discuss issues that are occurring in their own classroom experience. Preservice teachers can identify possible strategies for themselves so they will be prepared to deal with similar situations, and they can also begin to clarify how their understanding of pedagogy, educational theory, and their own teaching philosophy will translate into practice.

However the students are engaged in this text, it is important to allow them to wrestle with the issues on their own before hearing how an experienced teacher might have handled this situation. In their classroom setting, student teachers will have to make decisions and live with the results. They will have to use their own problem-solving strategies to make decisions about their work and their relationships with students and faculty. Students should be encouraged to unlayer the case and identify the multiple issues that are involved. Listing all of the embedded problems and perspectives on the board can help students see more clearly the complexity of teaching.

In addition, the exploration of several perspectives relating to the case is important, so that the student realizes that there is not just one way to handle situations that arise in the classroom. Along with discussion, role playing the position of the student teacher, cooperating teacher, or other involved parties may enable students to consider how they might respond when faced with that particular situation. Engaging pre-student teachers in a dialogue in which they speak as a participant in the case extends the learning to a "think-on-your-feet" experience and further assists with the development of critical thinking strategies.

This subsequent overview provides some suggestions for those who are unfamiliar with the use of cases in their classrooms.

Facilitating Case Discussions

1. Set clear expectations.
   a. What are the rules for participation?
   b. Does the classroom atmosphere foster risk taking?
   c. What are the goals/objectives for this session?
   d. How will you involve those who do not join in the conversation? Or will you?
2. Manage the time.
   a. With a case, there is always more to discuss than there is time, so set a time limit.
   b. Keep discussion focused on the objectives and the case.
   c. Allow for synthesis and bring discussion to closure.
3. Ask and encourage questions.
   a. Use open-ended questions: "What do you think is happening here?" "What would you do?"
   b. Ask for the facts.
   c. Ask for evidence to support ideas.
   d. Encourage curiosity: "How might you deal with this?
   e. Explore attitudes: "Why does this person (or the student think/respond/behave this way ... "

4. Listen.
   a. Silence is effective!
   b. Use wait time to allow students time to consider all possibilites.
   c. Limit giving your thoughts; allow student development of ideas.
5. Organize and Structure.
   a. Set the structure—whole class or small group interaction?
   b. Group roles? How will groups report to the whole class?
   c. Write key ideas and comments on the board or overhead.
   d. Synthesize: list options/idea for solving the problem on board, etc.
   e. Link the situation with theory and pedagogy that has been discussed in prior classes. Consider having faculty who teach the various pre-service courses facilitate cases that related to their subject matter.
   f. Follow up with activities or assignments (journaling, reflective response, further research).
6. Avoid common problems.
   a. Insufficient wait time.
   b. Rapid reward: "right" "good" to first answer offered.
   c. Programmed answers: avoid playing "guess what I am thinking."
   d. A classroom climate that discourages risk taking—avoid intimidation, numerous interruptions, etc.
   e. Closed questions.

Adapted from L. Wilkerson & J. Boehrer. (1992). *Using cases about teaching for faculty development. To improve the academy.* A publication of the Professional and Organizational Development Network in Higher Education.

ACKNOWLEDGMENTS

In the experience of every budding teacher there is much that can be learned and passed along to preservice teachers who have yet to begin their student teaching. I am grateful to the students who shared with me their stories of these initial experiences. Some gave me permission to use reflections they had generated during their student teaching semester; some participated in interview sessions; some wrote me lengthy letters. Some of these cases are generated from the student's viewpoint, and some are from my own perspective. All of the stories have been edited to ensure the anonymity of the students, teachers, and schools involved.

As a college supervisor, I lived the experiences presented in this book along with the student teachers as I observed them in action. I learned much about teaching while viewing the classroom through their eyes. I thank the following individuals specifically for allowing me to share their stories and perceptions, and also offer my appreciation to those whose experience, while not overtly stated, is imbedded within many of these tales: Cynthia Alhquist, Jonathan Buckley, Jim Van Cura, David Daniels, Chris Dantzscher, Marc Dissell, Mike Floersch, Sarah (Hood) Floersch, Romelle Gangl, Mike Huberty, Steve Jensen, Steve Lang, Amy Lewanovich, Eric Naess, Daryl Schwalm, Wayne Seavey, Amy Smalley, Michael Smalley, Julie Smith, Debra Stevens, and James Wood.

I would also like to thank the reviewers of this book: Sue Dauer, Western Oregon State College; Jeanine M. Dell'Olio, Hope College; Susan M. Hahn, Dominican College; William Ray Heitzmann, Villanova University; Karen Kusiak, Colby College; Diane W. Kyle, University of Louisville; and Judy Marrou, University of Texas.

REFERENCES

Berlinger, D. C. (1991, Spring). Educational psychology and pedagogical expertise: New findings and new opportunities for thinking about training. *Educational Psychologist, 24,* 145–155.

Merseth, K. (1992). Cases for decision making in teacher education. In Schulman, J. (Ed.) *Case methods in teacher education* (pp. 50–63). New York: Teachers College Press.

Pitton, D. (1994, September). Mentoring: The special needs of student teachers. *People and Education, 2,* 338–352.

Schon, D. A. (1987). *Educating the reflective practitioner.* San Francisco: Jossey-Bass.

Schulman, L. (1992). Toward a pedagogy of cases. In Schulman, J. (Ed.) *Case methods in teacher education* (pp. 1–30). New York: Teachers College Press.

Shor, I. (1987). A Freirean approach to the crisis in teacher education. In Shor, I. (Ed.) *Freire for the classroom* (pp. 7–32). Portsmouth, NH: Boynton/Cook.

Wilkerson, L. & Boehrer, L. (1992). Using cases about teaching for faculty development. *To Improve the Academy.* A publication of the Professional and Organizational Development Network in Higher Education.

Contents

Part One

Part One

EYEWITNESS ACCOUNTS

*Experiences from the perspective
of the student teacher …*

Chapter One

MEETING ALL OF THEIR NEEDS

SETTING

First Grade

FOCUS QUESTIONS

While reading this case, consider the following questions:

- How do you generate your lesson plans?
- What are some critical factors in your decisions about what to teach?

The first graders all looked so cute that first day of my student teaching. My cooperating teacher had me read to them during story time, and I loved all their expressions and how eager they were to sit by me. I couldn't wait until I was teaching!

I started out gradually, presenting a reading lesson from our Companion Reading series. This program pairs students who practice their reading of letter sounds and then basic words by "reading" to each other. I really wanted to focus on reading, so that was the class that I began teaching. Planning what I would say, the examples I would give, the questions I would ask was fun, and I spent several hours each night preparing for these initial lessons. My cooperating teacher looked over my lesson plans in the morning before class began, and she would offer some suggestions or let me know that the plan looked good. When I executed these plans, they never seemed to go exactly as I had envisioned them, but my continued efforts began to pay off.

I was a little annoyed when my college supervisor asked to see my lesson plans at our first meeting. I figured that they would be examined and graded like they'd been in our methods classes.

"I see that you have a description of what you will be doing and saying in reading class tomorrow, but I am not sure of your objectives. Do you have those listed somewhere?"

I sighed. "My cooperating teacher doesn't write out objectives, and she hasn't said that anything is wrong with the way I do these," I replied.

"Your cooperating teacher has been teaching for years and probably carries in her head the objectives for the lesson. I think that you need to be specific in your own plans so that you can see where you're headed with this lesson."

"Ok, sure. I'll work on that," I lied. If the classroom teacher did not expect objectives in my lesson, I certainly wasn't going to make more work for myself by trying to write out some educational jargon. I was here to learn to teach!

As the weeks went by, I gradually began to take responsibility for more classes. The leisurely evening planning process I had used before was not going to cut it anymore. I spent several hours each evening writing up my plans—and that was even without the additional time it would have taken to write objectives! When I took over the whole class at the fourth week of my experience, I looked out at the faces of the first graders and felt a little panicky. There were three children in the Chapter I program who were getting special help, but who were struggling with reading even the simplest words. Charlie and Maggie were being pulled out for the gifted program; they were reading way ahead of their grade level. And then there was Joe, who was mainstreamed into our class for a couple of hours a day, whose physical and mental disabilities limited what he could do in the class. How was I going to meet all their needs?

Part of my problem, I knew, was finding the time for my planning. I used the teachers manual and textbooks to shape my lessons, and that helped me plan more quickly. Still, after being with the kids all day, I often had only a few hours for planning before I had to race across town to my own class. The student teaching semester included the health/drug awareness course as an evening class to "round out" our credit hours so we carried a full load. I also was trying to squeeze in a few hours of work so I could pay for gas to get me to school and contribute my share of the rent. On top of that, my roommates, who were not in education, often went out at night, leaving me with my books. They usually came home late and woke me from my much-needed sleep. They didn't seem to realize that I had to get up early and be ready for a full day of teaching!

I still managed to generate lessons that my cooperating teacher okayed and that kept the kids busy and learning. It was tough having her out of the room all day and dealing with all of the issues on my own, but I felt good about how things were progressing. When my college supervisor came to observe again, he asked me how I was dealing with the differences between the students in my classes. I stammered that I was working on full-class instruction and that the "pull out" programs were assisting with the diversity. My supervisor looked over my lesson plans and said, "Do you think that if you were to write out your objectives for each of these different groups of learners you would have a clearer picture of what you could do to assist them?"

"It is difficult to plan for a full day of lessons in all the subjects, let alone create several additional individual plans," I answered. "I know what I expect from each child and how to get them to that point."

My supervisor said that I might find it working now, but that using the student teaching experience to build and enhance my skills was important. "You might find it more helpful in the long run to specify your objectives," he finished. I said nothing, but mentally dismissed this statement. I knew that I was getting all the experience I needed in planning!

A week later, during reading, I noticed that my "chapter" kids were really struggling. I hit upon the idea of pairing them with the "enriched" kids so they could hear the words read correctly and see some good readers at work. For the next few days, I continued this pairing, proud of myself for discovering an effective process. The next day, after watching me teach, my cooperating teacher asked me if I was going to continue to have Charlie and Maggie work with Tracy, Tasha, and Mike. "I think that the three are benefiting from this positive modeling," I replied, satisfied with myself.

"What about Charlie and Maggie?" Mrs. Hentges asked. "What are your objectives for them?"

"You haven't asked for objectives in my lessons before," I quickly replied. "I know what I want them to accomplish."

"That may be true for the majority of the class, but I wonder about Charlie and Maggie. Today, Charlie was really being silly when he worked with Tasha. I think he might be getting bored with all of the repetition when he reads so well already. And Maggie's mom called today to ask why her daughter always had to work with the "low" students. She wondered if Maggie might be given something to read that was more on her level, and get a chance to pair with someone whose reading skills didn't demand so much from her."

"But that's the benefit of being paired with the chapter kids," I said. "Maggie and Charlie are learning more by teaching—about getting along with other kids, about being helpful, about sharing their skills. . . . "

Mrs. Hentges interrupted me. "Are those your objectives?"

"I guess so. I want them to be able to work together."

"But is that the only outcome for your reading classes?"

"No, I want all of the children to improve their word attack skills and comprehension level."

"Ok," Mrs. Hentges went on. "While your initial objectives may address valuable social skills, we still need to address their reading. I know I don't write out my objectives, but I am constantly thinking about each child and how to maximize their learning. Are Joe and Maggie getting an opportunity to improve if they always work with students who are quite a bit below their own reading level?"

"Probably not."

"And are they ready to read literature beyond the Companion Reading Series?"

"Sure."

"I agree. Another point is that I am not so sure that Tracy, Tasha, and Mike always appreciate the talents of Charlie and Maggie. Maybe we could put the three of them with students closer to their own abilities so they don't feel so 'outclassed' all the time." Mrs. Hentges smiled and went on. "You are good with the children, but you need to have a clear picture of 'why' you are doing something in the classroom. I haven't said anything about this issue before because your pairing of these different ability students is a good idea for the short term. However, I think we need to clarify what our goals are for all the students, so that we can decide if the pairs are working or if we need to vary our approach. I think we'll be in for a lot of unrest and disruption if we don't allow for Charlie and Maggie to work at their own level some of the time. We must be able to meet the needs of all of our students."

I sat silently. My lovely lesson plans—all that work . . . But I had to admit that I didn't really know why I was doing some of the things I had written down. I hadn't really thought beyond the "keep them busy and keep them involved" stage of planning. I had been planning for what I thought was the "average" kid. I thought using the teacher's manual would help me avoid problems, but the diversity of student abilities wasn't really addressed. I wondered about Joe. I had made sure that his mainstreamed time in class was always during storytime and recess. This had made things easy for me, but I wondered if I ought to have some specific reason for why this was occurring.

The next day when we looked over my plans, Mrs. Hentges again pointed out that I was ready to begin focusing on the rationale behind my lessons. "You have a good communication style, you are knowledgeable, and you are very aware of what the children are doing during class," she said. "It's time to move to a higher level of awareness of your students' needs." She helped me by asking me why I was having the kids complete certain tasks, by getting me to voice the purpose of my lessons and activities. We regrouped for reading, putting Joe and Maggie together, and gave them several books to read to each other. During our large-group reading, I identified several students who were reading well but were closer to Tracy, Tasha, and Mike's ability level. When these groups got going, all the children were more focused and seemed to be improving their reading ability. I still wanted to work on social skills, but I clarified that this wasn't my only objective. I realized that I had used the "social skills" objective to justify my grouping. I needed to address specific academic objectives for all students, not just general goals like "keeping the students busy."

I also realized that I hadn't considered what my objectives were for Joe. He needed to learn to interact with other children his own age and to listen and communicate more clearly. When I thought about it, using story time to engage him and all the children in conversation about the book was a good method, and it allowed me to work on one of the objectives from his IEP, which stated that "Joe was to practice communicating his thoughts appropriately and clearly to peers."

The second half of my placement is going to be in the fifth grade. I realize that I will have to be more specific in defining my objectives and figure out how to deal with the issue of planning time. My new cooperating teacher mentioned that I would be able to write the end of the quarter test for social studies. He said, "As long as you have clear objectives, you have a guide for how you will teach and a plan for assessing the children. Your test should tell whether or not the children have met the objectives."

I am wondering if the test should be the same for all of the kids. What if I have students like Tracy, Tasha, and Mike? Should they be expected to "pass" a test when their reading ability might affect their score? What about high achievers? Should they have a more challenging test? Would a project that asked the students to use their knowledge be a better indicator of what they knew than a paper-and-pencil test? And if I have mainstreamed students with IEPs, will they even be expected to learn social studies? Why would I even teach social studies to someone like Joe? This is certainly more complicated than I realized! I may need to get the special education teacher to help me out. It's becoming clear that I need to work on getting the "why" before the "what" in my planning.

My college supervisor told me this analogy: Objectives provide a road map so students and the teacher don't get lost. It makes sense to me now. I have to make the time to think through what my expectations are for all of my students and then generate lessons that help them meet their goal. I just hope I have time for all of this!

◎ POINTS TO PONDER

1. How can classroom teachers plan appropriate objectives for all of their students?

2. How will you balance your life with the time required for planning effective lessons during student teaching?

3. How closely linked should objectives, lesson plans, and assessment be in the classroom?

4. Given all of the expectations placed on teachers in the classroom, do you think it is possible for teachers to meet all of their students' needs?

5. Should a beginning teacher go about the tasks of teaching in the same manner as an experienced teacher?

6. What are the advantages and disadvantages of using teaching manuals and texts to plan lessons?

FURTHER READING

Borko, H., & Niles, J. A. (1987). Descriptions of teacher planning: Ideas for teachers and researchers. In V. Richardson-Koehler (Ed.), *Educators' handbook: A research perspective* (pp. 167—187). New York: Longman.

Cangelosi, J. (1992). *Systematic teaching strategies.* White Plains, NY: Longman.

Henak, R. (1984). *Lesson planning for meaningful variety in teaching.* Washington, DC: National Education Association.

Lewis, R., & Doorlag, D. (1991). *Teaching special students in the mainstream* (3rd ed.). Upper Saddle River, NJ: Merrill/Prentice Hall.

Mager, R. (1984). *Preparing instructional objectives* (2nd rev. ed.). Palo Alto, CA: D. S. Lake.

McCarthy, B. (1980, 1987). *The 4MAT system, teaching to learning styles with right/left mode techniques.* Barrington, IL: EXCELL, Inc.

Yinger, R. (1980). A study of teacher planning. *The Elementary School Journal, 80,* 107–127.

Chapter Two

GETTING TO KNOW MYSELF

SETTING

High School Literature Classes

FOCUS QUESTIONS

While reading this case, consider the following questions:

- How quickly do you expect to develop a high level of comfort with this teaching experience?
- How will you keep students focused on your lesson?

Oh God!" I thought. "I can't do this! . . . For as long as I can remember, I have wanted to be a teacher. And now? . . . Now I don't think I can do it." My waterbed gently rocked as I lay in total darkness. No tears escaped my eyes, but I felt empty and depressed—like a total failure.

It was midway through my student teaching experience and I had just lost control of my first class. Today during my fifth hour English literature class I had said, "Be quiet," and they had kept on talking. I had said, "Sit down," and they had stood. I had said, "You owe me five minutes after class," and they had laughed. "God," I prayed, "why did you let me spend all of these years pursuing something so absolutely horrible?" All of the troubles I had experienced so far were nothing compared to this day.

The first difficulty I encountered when I began my student teaching was the daily schedule. Getting up at five in the morning was a real shock to my system. My body enjoyed staying up until midnight and waking at what I had thought was a respectable time: eight or nine o'clock the next morning. Staying in one location for the entire day was also rough. My days prior to student teaching usually consisted of a couple of hours of classes, three or four hours of work, and then several hours of homework to finish the day. Plenty of time for myself was included in each day. Now I felt like I never had enough time for anything: to think, or sleep, or even prepare my lessons as carefully as I would have liked. I found that being in the school building for a whole day felt weird and confining. So even the easiest part of teaching—just physically being there—was stressing me out!

The actual classroom experience was another story. I, who had been confident as a student, was a nervous wreck in front of my tenth-grade English class. I talked too fast. My nervousness caused me to slip up, and when I made an error, I felt embarrassed . . . doubly so if a student recognized the mistake before I did. When I gave my first lecture, my master teacher, Eileen, seemed in agony as she watched me. She later told me that she had felt that some of the students could have done a better job than I on that first day! She left me alone many of those first days I was teaching. I was only handling one class, but I had no one but myself to rely on for help. Whenever a student talked out of turn, I worried that he or she was being disrespectful or that I was losing control. During those first few weeks, I felt tired, anxious, worried, and depressed. I saw the next 15 weeks stretched out before me as an endless sea of frustration.

One of my first mistakes was that I tried to be friends with the students. I didn't want to be an overbearing ogre of a teacher, like some I remembered from my childhood. It didn't take me long to realize that the students had their own friends. They didn't need me. It was hard to struggle with the realization that I was no longer the student. As a teacher, I had to make friends with the other teachers. Fortunately, I began to adapt to my new surroundings. Time was my helpmate—I just gradually became used to the schedule, the students, my surroundings, and the other teachers. Slowly, I began to relax in my classes. In time, I found friendships among my colleagues. Finally, I began to gain a little confidence.

Up to this point, my classes had been upper-level students. Phase 2 began after five weeks at my school, when I added my master teacher's "regular" fifth-hour class. This sophomore English class would be reading *Julius Caesar*, and I would be presenting this unit. Another fear loomed ahead—I barely understood Shakespeare. My preparation had focused on contemporary literature . . . how was I going to teach Shakespeare? Eileen stayed in the room during the first few days of the new unit. She looked over my lessons and said that they were well organized. When she said that I had improved immeasurably, I filled with pride. "This isn't too bad," I thought. The students were quiet and polite. One student even told me that she liked the way I was teaching the play. My heart swelled. "I'm a teacher! I'm a teacher!" I sang to myself. Things flowed smoothly for about two weeks, and then came the dark day that left me praying for an end to this torture.

My students had been assigned a study guide as homework. (If nothing else, I did have good lesson plans. I tried to fill every minute so they would be "on task" and not cause problems.) My lesson for that day was to go through that guide and correct them. Perhaps one of my mistakes was entering the class with the thought that if anyone got out of line I would "nail" them. Eileen had said I needed to be more firm, so I vowed that today was the day I would make sure the students toed the line. There were four young men who had been restless during the first part of the week. Today, Friday, I was going to "get" them. As we progressed through the study guide, a young man made a smart comment. I told him he would have to stay after class for five minutes.

"What?" he said.

"You're talking when you should be quiet."

"Bacon," another student said, very deliberately.

"OK," I said to the new heckler, "you also owe me five minutes after class."

"You're kidding?" he retorted. "For saying 'bacon'?"

At that moment, I lost my class. No one listened to me, and the two students in question certainly did not stay after class as I had requested. When I told Eileen, she offered what comfort she could and told me to go home and forget about it. She said that we would start out with a clean slate next week. (She told me later that she had been afraid that I would never come back.) So . . . this is how I came to be lying on my bed praying for an end to my torment.

The next week things went downhill. The students were never as bad as they had been my first day in the classroom, but I had little control. I tried giving the fifth-period class a long and difficult homework assignment. That didn't work. It just gave *me* more papers to correct, and it didn't seem to bother the students that they received more work as a punishment for their behavior. I tried a point system where I docked daily points for inappropriate behavior, but the students tried competing to see who could get the most in one day. I tried a number of things, but nothing seemed to work. Eileen thought that the reason things went poorly was because I had begun to expect this class to be "off the wall." The students were enacting the self-fulfilling prophecy I had given them—that they were not ever going to listen to me. I stopped expecting them to.

There were two things my master teacher did at this point that helped me begin to break the pattern I had established and gain control of my class. First, we did some role playing. She would model how I should enter the classroom, what I should say to begin the class, and how I should respond to student comments. Then she would play the student and I would try to duplicate her comments and actions. Practicing what I was going to say and what I expected from the students in my "class from hell" helped me immeasurably. Secondly, we talked about my "presence" in the room. She had observed that as I got angry or frustrated my voice began to rise. I needed to speak in a deeper voice, project more and fake some confidence. Finally, one Friday, my class actually responded to me! They were perfect! When I told them to take 20 minutes to read, they settled down and did it. I was stunned. When I went to the teacher's lounge for lunch I looked at Eileen and said, "Fifth hour listened to me. They were actually good! They were quiet and worked hard."

She answered, "See, you are improving! If you go in there with confidence, they'll listen." This was one of the days my college advisor had been to the school to observe me during an earlier class, and I had been pumped up with confidence from the pep talk she had given me. Eileen continued, "The difference with fifth hour today was that you went in there feeling confident after your conference with your advisor. Confidence makes all the difference."

She was right. During my final weeks with fifth hour, the class was very well behaved. Part of the reason was that Eileen team-taught with me some and thus was in the room more. But that wasn't the whole reason. When Eileen had observed me earlier, the students had been rowdy despite her presence. I could actually feel a difference in my attitude toward teaching the young people in this class. I felt confident. My plans began to be less prescriptive and include some group interactions and discussion. (I had been afraid to use anything but teacher-directed methods up to now.) On my last day, one of the students who had been a real pain said to me, "You did good!" Once I had left, he told my master teacher, "She was a pretty good teacher, she'll do ok." I almost cried when Eileen told me this. Even thinking about it now, I feel teary.

The completion of my student teaching experience left me exhausted and happy. I learned more about my personal strengths and weaknesses during this semester than at any other time of my life. I know that I am well organized and I am feeling more comfortable using student-centered techniques. I still have to work on communicating a sense of confidence to my students.

I don't know what the future holds. I am not sure that I really want to work as hard as I did during this experience. Maybe an office job, with fewer interpersonal interactions is a more comfortable place for me to be. Still, I spent all this money on my education, and I know that I like teaching—when it's going well!

Whatever I decide, I know that I have grown tremendously from this experience. I can continue to learn and be an effective teacher—I just have to decide if that is what I really want.

POINTS TO PONDER

1. What do you see as the major problems this young teacher faced? Can you identify what might have caused these difficulties for her in the classroom?

2. The student teacher in this story had a preconceived view of herself in the classroom that affected her ability to teach. What are your fears and expectations as you approach student teaching? How would you rate your confidence level? What can you do to alleviate any concerns you might have?

3. Discuss the relationship between the student teacher and her cooperating teacher. How did this affect her teaching? What kind of a relationship do you want to have with your cooperating teacher? What will you do to ensure that this occurs?

4. If you found yourself in a situation where you felt that you had "lost the class" what would you do? What resources are available for you during student teaching to help you address difficulties that you may encounter?

5. How did student teaching affect this preservice teacher's personal life? What relationship is there between your personal life and your professional life? What adjustments in your life might you need to make to ensure you don't experience similar difficulties?

6. Discuss the use of student-centered and teacher-centered methodologies. Should this student teacher have used different strategies like cooperative learning earlier in her experience?

FURTHER READING

Dollase, R. H. (1992). *Voices of beginning teachers: Visions and realities.* New York: Teachers College Press.

Lieberman, A., & Miller, L. (1984). *Teachers, their world and their work.* Alexandria, VA: Association for Supervision and Curriculum Development.

Schubert, W. H., & Ayers, W. C. (Eds.). (1992). *Teacher lore: learning from our own experience.* New York: Longman.

Sprick, R. (1985). *Discipline in the secondary classroom: A problem-by-problem survival guide.* West Nyack, NY: The Center for Applied Research in Education, Inc.

Chapter 3

I WANT TO BE ALONE

SETTING

Third Grade

FOCUS QUESTION

While reading this case, consider the following question:

⬤ How much support do you want and expect from a cooperating teacher?

As I stuffed the pile of papers left to grade in my briefcase, I thought back over the past few weeks. Ever since I had begun my student teaching experience in Mrs. Clark's third-grade classroom, I knew that I had made the right career choice. I loved seeing the excitement for learning in the eyes of my students, and the fact that I was planning and providing the lessons that created this excitement was very satisfying.

I had known that Mrs. Clark was a dedicated professional, and her high standards for planning and bringing outside information to her teaching was well known. I had heard about her from other preservice teachers who had worked in her building and I knew that she would be a knowledgeable guide for my student teaching. When I went to interview with her prior to getting assigned to her room, we hit it off right away. Mrs. Clark made it very clear that she had high expectations for students (and student teachers!) and that she provided many resources and materials for her classes beyond the textbooks and prescribed curriculum. I was excited by this, because the creative aspect of teaching was what had drawn me to the elementary classroom.

The first few weeks we team-taught, with Mrs. Clark laying out the lesson and me presenting several parts or leading small groups. I taught several reading lessons using puppets that Mrs. Clark had made, read to the children during storytime, and set up science stations that blended my ideas and Mrs. Clark's. The two of us seemed to click in the classroom, and I felt I was well on my way to becoming a teacher. She would make a comment, and I would add to it, and between us we seemed to be able to get all the children on task and working effectively. Mrs. Clark was excited about my ideas for an interactive bulletin board for math, and I loved expanding on the ideas for group work that she had previously used in the classroom.

When my college supervisor came to observe me after a few weeks, she commented on my teaching and pointed out that one of my strengths was my ability to use the students' knowledge to build a base for my lessons. I told her about a math lesson I was preparing using manipulatives, and I mentioned that I was going to take sole responsibility for all subjects beginning the following week. When my college supervisor asked if I would be alone in the room, Mrs. Clark piped up, "No, I think it is best for me to be there to assist if there are any problems. I don't want to abandon her at this point." At the time, it seemed wise to have my cooperating teacher there as a backup.

The next two weeks passed quickly. I was busy writing lessons and teaching, and I found that the children really responded to my interactive style of teaching. Things were going well, although I was anxious to have the children all to myself, to really feel that I was the teacher. Every day, Mrs. Clark sat in the back of the room at her desk, greeting the children as they came and went and smiling encouragement to me from the sidelines. As the days wore on however, I noticed that if I made a slight error or wasn't as quick to get to the point, she would politely interrupt and add the necessary information. If the children came to her with a question or note from home, she'd say, "I'll just take care of this so you don't have to worry about it." I knew that she was being supportive, assisting me so I wouldn't make any major errors, but I was beginning to feel that I wasn't measuring up to her standards. I wanted to do it all—and I felt confident that I could be successful. I realized that I wasn't as skilled as Mrs. Clark, but she had been teaching for eight years. I knew that, while I might not be as smooth in my delivery or anticipate every possible student response, I was a good beginning teacher. As I gathered my papers for the trip home, I decided to speak to my college supervisor about this issue.

Later, during our phone conversation, Dr. McIntyre listened to my comments, then paused and asked, "What is your major concern regarding Mrs. Clark's presence in the classroom?"

"I feel really funny complaining about Mrs. Clark," I replied. "She has been very helpful, offered me the use of all of her files, and she's been positive and encouraging of my original lessons. We worked together so well, and I know her close scrutiny the first few weeks helped me sharpen my skills and fine-tune my lessons."

"Do you think that Mrs. Clark is uncertain about your teaching skills?" Dr. McIntyre asked.

"No . . . it's funny really. I have so much respect for her and I know that she sees me as a colleague. We meet every morning before school to go over my plans and discuss how the lessons went the day before, and usually things are fine. It's just that she always has one or two changes that she'd like me to make. They're not major issues, but she always suggests some way that I should change the lesson just a bit. I never seem to get it completely right. Things were great when we collaborated on lessons early on, but now that I'm handling things on my own, it seems that she is always hovering in the background, waiting for me to goof. I know that I'm not perfect, but I don't even get the chance to correct my own little slips before she is chiming in from the gallery."

"I wonder," Dr. McIntyre mused, "if maybe Mrs. Clark is feeling a bit uncomfortable because you are so effective."

"What do you mean?"

"You have developed a rapport with the children; they look to you as much as to Mrs. Clark for leadership in the classroom. You said yourself that you collaborated effectively. There is a bond, a sense of community that forms in good classrooms between the students and the teacher. It might be that your effectiveness is generating some discomfort for Mrs. Clark because she is, in effect 'losing' her children, her class, to you."

"What should I do about that? I want to be seen as the teacher. I think that this is the only way that I can really test myself and challenge myself to fulfill the role. The way things are now, I'm not sure that kids are listening and responding to me or if their interest is due to Mrs. Clark's presence. She is still connected to the class. I guess what I really want is to be left alone in the classroom to see if I can manage things and teach effectively on my own."

"Okay," Dr. McIntyre replied. "You have a valid concern. But you do need to realize that Mrs. Clark is the official teacher, and you are, in essence, a guest in her class. I think you ought to talk to Mrs. Clark and let her know how you feel."

"Well, that's just it, Dr. McIntyre. I feel like that would be undermining the relationship that we have established. I know that she's just trying to help."

"If you feel this strongly about the issue, I think that it is worth discussing. Why don't I come over tomorrow and sit in on your morning conference? Perhaps I can steer the conversation toward a discussion of your 'solo' work in the class."

"That'd be great! See you at 7:00!"

The next morning I was early for our meeting. I told Mrs. Clark that Dr. McIntyre was joining us, and she seemed fine with that. After listening to us going through the day's plans, Dr. McIntyre spoke.

"It seems that you two work very well together."

"Oh yes," Mrs. Clark replied, " Terry is a very good beginning teacher. I find that there is very little that I have to correct in her planning or teaching."

"So you think that she should try it on her own?" Dr. McIntyre asked.

"Well she is—I just help her see where she could improve things a bit."

"So do you leave her alone in the room?"

"Well, I think it's best to be available to offer support and to be available in case something goes wrong," Mrs. Clark replied. "I am responsible for the class, you know."

Later that day, Dr. McIntyre called me to comment on the morning meeting. "I really think that Mrs. Clark sees her behavior as supportive, Terry. You are a fine beginning teacher."

"I know that. It just doesn't seem that Mrs. Clark really believes it, or she would be willing to let me handle the class on my own. You heard her—she is always nit-picking. I think she looks for things to 'correct' about my teaching. I have yet to have a lesson she hasn't wanted me to change in some small way."

"The way I see it," Dr. McIntyre continued, "is that you have several choices. You can use Mrs. Clark's suggestions to gain even more insight into effective teaching. She is, as you have said, a very organized and inspiring teacher. Another option is to tell Mrs. Clark how you feel and try to come to an understanding, or you can just let it go."

"Let it go?"

"Yes. It is, after all, Mrs. Clark's classroom. And while you are getting a wonderful chance to learn how to teach and to get feedback from a skilled educator, she is the one who is ultimately responsible for the class. You may feel like she is hovering over you, but that is her perception of the role of a cooperating teacher. So unless you are willing to let her know how you feel, then I think you'll just need to grin and bear it."

"I wouldn't want to upset Mrs. Clark. She will be writing my final evaluation and recommendation for my placement file, after all. And I really do value her help and insights. I just feel so torn about this issue." I thought for a while, then sighed, conceding to Dr. McIntyre's suggestion. "I guess, in the long run, this isn't that big of a thing."

"In your career you will have to make decisions about your relationship with other teachers and administrators all the time. You'll need to decide which battles are worth fighting and which are best to just let go. You'll also have many occasions when supervisors will be watching you teach and providing you with feed-back about your teaching. How will you deal with that?"

I grinned. "I guess this is one of those 'learning opportunities' you talked about in class, huh, Dr. McIntyre?"

"Well, you do have the opportunity to learn something about relationships in schools and how you will respond in situations that are similar to this."

I nodded. "I really would like to be left on my own in the classroom. It bugs me to have her looking over my shoulder all the time. But I'm not sure if I'm ready to ask her to leave. I've got a few more weeks to let things play out. I'll keep you posted, Dr. McIntyre. Maybe if I try not to let her presence and little comments bother me, I will be able to let this issue drop. This is one of those deci-sions that only I can make, and I'm not sure it's worth irritating someone who's been as helpful as Mrs. Clark."

◎ POINTS TO PONDER

1. What should a student teacher's skill level be before taking sole responsibility for a class during the student teaching experience?

2. How influential do you think your cooperating teacher will be on your meth-ods of teaching? Why or why not?

3. Should your goal be to satisfy your cooperating teacher and meet all of his/her expectations? Why or why not?

4. How important is honest communication between cooperating teacher and stu-dent teacher? Should you reveal all of your thoughts, feelings, and concerns?

5. How important is the letter of recommendation that your cooperating teacher will write? What can/will you do if this letter is not as positive or sup-portive as you would like it to be?

6. What role does the college supervisor play in the relationship between the student teacher and the cooperating teacher?

◎ FURTHER READING

Blumberg, A. (1980). *Supervisors and teachers: A private cold war* (2nd ed.). Berkeley CA: McCutchan.

Gold, Y. (1992). Psychological support for mentors and beginning teachers: A criti-cal dimension. In T. Bey & C. T. Holmes (Eds.), *Mentoring—Contemporary prin-ciples and issues* (pp. 25–34). Reston, VA: Association of Teacher Educators.

Pitton, D. (1994). Mentoring: The special needs of student teachers. *People and education: The human side of schools*, 2(3), 338–352.

Waite, D. (1993). Teachers in conference: A qualitative study of teacher-supervisor face-to-face interactions. *American Educational Research Journal*, 30(4), 675–702.

Weiss, C., Cambone, J., & Wyeth, A. (1992). Trouble in paradise: Teacher conflicts in shared decision making. *Educational Administration Quarterly*, 28(3), 350–367.

Zonca, P. (1973). A case study exploring the effects on an intern teacher of the condition of openness in a clinical supervisory relationship. (Unpublished Ph.D. dissertation, University of Pittsburgh, 1973.) *Dissertation Abstracts International*, 33, 658–659A.

Chapter Four

MEETING THEM WHERE THEY ARE

SETTING

High School History

FOCUS QUESTIONS

While reading this case, consider the following questions:

- How do you generate lessons that engage students?
- Do you consider yourself a "student-centered" teacher or a "content-centered" teacher?

The first day I was observed by my college supervisor during my student teaching semester was a lesson I also chose to videotape. Although this was a requirement mandated by my college, I really wanted to get a picture of myself teaching. I had been teaching for a few weeks already, and for this class, a senior-level elective in American history that focused on the conflicts that shaped our society, I had researched, developed, and implemented what I thought was a very interesting lesson on the Red Baron. Reviewing the tape, my level of inexperience was clear to me, and so was the students' lack of interest!

By design, I intended my Red Baron lesson to be a chance for me to "shine" in front of everyone. My hopes were very high. However, the impact of several things dulled my shining moment, and these were easy to see while viewing the tape. First, I had purposefully taped the third-hour class, which has been very lethargic during the semester, expecting that everyone would be turned on and very involved with this exciting lesson. This was certainly not the case. Although I had been very enthusiastic in presenting the material, when the camera panned the classroom, the bored looks, yawns, and limited number of note-takers made it obvious that my excitement did not transfer to my students. And I hadn't even noticed what the students were doing! Second, when I asked questions and heard "I dunno" several times in response to my queries, it was obvious by my tone and facial expression that I was frustrated and a bit irritated at the students' lack of participation. Perhaps as a result of this, I began to call on only my "reliable" students, limiting involvement in the discussion to a very few individuals.

I was very surprised at what occurred, because I loved my Red Baron lesson. I had read artifacts-excerpts from his journal that identified this fighter pilot's personal side, and I had read them to the class, attempting to convey the intense tone of the writing by my vocal inflection. I had asked students to give a comparison of the Baron's private reflections on the war with his "bigger than life" persona. This discussion of the struggles that a participant in an earlier war felt could be related to the traumas felt by Vietnam veterans later in the semester—or at least, that is what I had planned. After watching the looks of indifference on the faces of the students in my class as I went on and on about this one figure from history, and seeing how I failed to involve and motive the majority of the class, I began to reevaluate my approach to teaching.

Conversations with my cooperating teacher and my college supervisor made me face a problem I never thought I would encounter: a seeming inability for students to find meaningfulness in the material. My college supervisor asked, "Why is this information important to the lives of those students in your class?" I had thought that because the Red Baron appeared on the upcoming test, and because this concept could be tied together with later information, and because *I* enjoyed the material, that the kids would too. History had been my true love, and while I had often studied because "it was required," or something was "sure to be on the test," I also found the interactions and personalities of the past intriguing. Yet somehow it seemed so meaningless to these urban kids. I was a bit irked that something I felt so strongly about, and on which I had spent so much time and energy, was such a bomb in the classroom.

As I sat and thought about my lesson, I had to acknowledge that one of the reasons I had been excited about the lesson was because my father had been in the Air Force, and I loved planes. I thought that my lesson would personalize the experiences of the war for my students, but perhaps those connections were all in my mind. What had I done to find out about the students' interests? Had I communicated to them the reasons that I found the journals of the Red Baron so interesting? How could I "meet the students where they were" in regard to their knowledge and interest in history? One thing seemed certain, I needed to ask the students about their own knowledge of a subject rather than assuming that they knew nothing about our lesson.

After some prodding from my supervisor, I decided that I had to spend some time searching for ideas that related our study of history to the students' lives. Prior to that, I needed to take some time to find out a bit more about the class as individuals. Because I had been "turned on" to history by my own background, I decided to have the students interview someone from their family who had been in the service or to get their opinion about the service if they knew no one who was a veteran. They would then give brief presentations in class.

In addition, I decided that I needed to give the class reasons identifying why each lesson should be important to them (beyond just knowing it for the test). I also needed to acknowledge that what was inherently exciting to me, might not be as thought provoking for the students. I realized that I had to generate a connection, or reason for their interest, to avoid ending up frustrated and blaming the students for their lack of involvement. I also knew that I needed to identify for my class what it was that the students were expected to know and do after completing a unit—whether it was to identify names and dates, or compare and contrast two different time periods. The thing is, I had been so engrossed in developing this wonderful lesson to present, on giving my class the benefit of my expertise, that I forgot to consider some of the very basic things that I knew were important for the students.

The tape had also pointed out that my ability to lead a discussion needed some fine-tuning. I decided that rather than generate questions spontaneously (which I thought would lead to a more student-directed discussion), I would write out specific questions ahead of time. Another look at the tape pointed out that I needed to give the students more time to generate their answers. I also read over my textbook on cooperative learning and realized that I had not attempted any method of instruction other than a teacher-centered, direct-instruction approach. With this fact in mind, I planned to put the students in small groups and have them generate answers to my prompts prior to our whole-class discussion. I hoped that this would give everyone some time to think about the questions and hear various viewpoints from their peers. And finally, I decided to use a seating chart to mark which students had participated in our class discussions and to keep track of this, so that I could direct questions or elicit responses from students who typically did not answer in class. As I looked at the "action plan" that my supervisor and I had outlined, I wondered, "Would all of this work?" I was still a bit uncomfortable about "giving up control" of the classroom and using cooperative learning. Still, I wanted to get the students involved in their own learning. I was sure glad that I had 10 weeks left of my student teaching—because all of this would certainly take some time!

 ## POINTS TO PONDER

1. Respond to the comment that this teacher made that he needed to "meet the students where they were." Do you think that his plan of action will help him meet this goal? Why or why not?

2. This student teacher identified several areas to work on during the remainder of his experience. Identify these and comment on whether you think his plan to deal with these issues will be effective. What else might he do to achieve his goals? Were there any concerns that you feel were not addressed by the student teacher?

3. How do you feel about videotaping yourself during student teaching? What benefits do you see from taping your teaching? What arrangements can you make for using this as a tool to assist in your development? How could you use a second, or multiple, tapings?

4. How will you feel if your supervisor points out that you have many issues to address in your development? Do you think it is feasible to make these changes within the time of your student teaching experience? What will you do throughout your career to continue your professional development?

5. This teacher acknowledges that he felt frustrated when his students didn't respond to his lesson as he had anticipated. Do you think that you might also feel this way in a similar situation? How can you deal with these feelings of frustration? Do you think this student teacher's plan will eliminate further frustration?

6. Do you think this student teacher needs to involve the students more in making decisions in the classroom? Should the class be focused on what the students are interested in, or should lessons be determined by the teacher's interest and background?

7. What is your philosophical approach to the classroom? Would you say that you focus on content or students? How does this focus affect your teaching?

✺ FURTHER READING

Bateman, W. L. (1990). *Open to question: The art of teaching and learning by inquiry.* San Francisco: Jossey-Bass Publishers.

Kierstead, J. (1986). How teachers manage individual and small group work in active classrooms. *Educational Leadership,* 44(2) 22–25.

Hawkins, M. L., & Graham, M. D. (1994). *Curriculum architecture.* Columbus, OH: National Middle School Association.

Purkey, W. W., & Stanley, P. H. (1991). *Invitational teaching, learning and living.* Washington, DC: National Education Association.

Chapter Five

TO BE OR NOT TO BE . . .

SETTING

Middle School Language Arts

FOCUS QUESTIONS

While reading this case, consider the following questions:

- What goals do you have for yourself during student teaching?
- What personal attributes enable you to be effective in the classroom?

I went into this experience of student teaching with several questions and came out with answers. I wanted to know if my philosophy of teaching would change. I wanted to know if my version of classroom management would work, or if my class would be a zoo. Finally, I wanted to figure out if I really wanted to be a teacher. I got answers to all three questions. Now if someone would just lend me a teacher's secret decoder ring so I could figure out what it all means . . .

The first, and perhaps biggest, question I had was whether or not my philosophy of education would hold water in the "real world." I think that I began formulating my philosophy when I was in high school. I came from a very unstable family. My dad was a violent alcoholic, and my mom was chronically depressed. I spent a lot of time looking out for my sisters and cleaning up after my parents because they were too absorbed in their own mess to parent. For me, school was a haven because I could think about things that had nothing to do with my family, and the only person I was responsible for was myself. When I began teaching this semester, I really wanted to create a sense of community in my classroom so students would feel safe. I felt that not only would the students get a chance to relax a little, but they might feel more comfortable in expressing themselves both verbally and in writing if the classroom environment was more like a community. I found that this was true, at least to a certain extent. As part of their poetry unit I gave the students the option to write and explain their own poems. They could also choose to analyze song lyrics, compare several poems, or create their own projects. An overwhelming number chose to write their own poems. I couldn't believe some of the things these kids wrote. They described rage at their second-class citizenship as students. They expressed frustration with the racism in their school. They vented about jealousy and their friendships. They were very up front and honest in their explanations. I cried when I read a few of them. Knowing that they felt they could share such personal feelings with me made me realize that my philosophy was working.

The second part of my philosophy that I wanted to experiment with was the idea that curriculum material should relate to the students' lives and, wherever possible, be student directed. Fortunately, I was assigned to a team of two teachers who constantly tried to weave the student's interests and issues into their language arts curriculum. I got to see these ideas in action and try them almost daily. My cooperating teachers chose a lot of material to teach that had some direct relation to the lives of the students, or at least was interesting to them, and they also incorporated into the lessons material that was created entirely by the students themselves. We didn't stick to traditional literature, and we did a lot of fun and creative things to break up the pattern of reading, writing, listening, and speaking.

The team teaching approach was also new to me, but in addition to observing this approach, I got to put it into practice by co-teaching a unit with another student teacher. This made my first "solo" teaching much more comfortable. We decided that it would be fun to try a science fiction unit. The students were very energetic, creative, and bored, and consequently they looked like they were going to be the fabled student teacher "behavior nightmare." Most of them were very excited about the science fiction unit, partially because science fiction isn't usually taught as a viable, respected form of literature, and they felt as if they were getting away with something by studying it. We made a point of giving them a lot of options, both creative and concrete, in an effort to make sure that we could reach as many students as possible with each assignment. They were a particularly active, dramatic bunch, so we included exercises in which they could write and act out their own scenes. We also set up a semidemocratic system in class where the students could voice their opinions openly, without (much) fear of retribution, as long as they stayed within some respectful guidelines. This experiment in particular paid off. The class was probably a lot noisier than most, but we got constant feedback and could adjust what we were doing and what direction we were taking the class. I also think the students felt as though they had more of an investment in the class. They still didn't get everything turned in on time, but the attitude of the class in general improved incredibly.

My second big question, whether or not my classroom management would be successful, was probably the one I agonized over the most. I felt like an emotional fruitcake for a lot of my time as a student teacher, and this question was the reason. I am a fairly quiet, soft-spoken person. I don't like to yell at anyone unless there are no other options. I also like to be casual with the students. I asked them to call me by my first name, and I tried to not to speak down to them to diminish the power differential. Most of the time I found these tactics successful. If students were talking, I'd ask them to be quiet without raising my voice. I would go up to the student's desk to quiet him or her, and the one-on-one contact usually worked. I felt I got a lot of honest answers from students and that they were willing to talk in class and give feedback because I spoke to them respectfully. However, I couldn't stop asking myself if this quiet approach would work when the students were really determined to be troublesome.

My quiet nature was the crux of a huge problem I had with my student teammate. She was very outgoing, assertive, and competitive. She also had a fabulous voice that carried far. It was easy for her to discipline someone at the other end of our classroom. She could raise her voice slightly and be heard down the hall. One day she took me aside and told me that she felt like the "bad guy" in the class because she was "doing all of the disciplining." I answered that I felt as though I was doing a lot too, but that because our styles were different, hers louder and mine quieter, hers was the most noticeable. So, I tried to be louder after that and more assertive in class because I didn't want her to take the brunt of the students' animosity. I discovered that I just couldn't keep it up, and that her "loud" approach wasn't as effective for me because my voice wasn't as strong as hers. Calling out across the room just didn't fit my personality.

As the semester wore on, I began to doubt myself a lot. If I couldn't holler at someone across the room, maybe I just didn't have what it took to keep my class under control. I began to examine why it was so hard for me to be loud. I could be loud enough when I was on stage and had been in plays and outdoor productions where the audience heard me just fine. I decided that I just didn't want to be a loud disciplinarian but couldn't fathom why it bothered me so much. I figured that it had to have something to do with my background and decided that it must be because in some circumstances silence is simply equal to survival. I spent a lot of time hiding from my Dad; being quiet is a big part of remaining unseen. The stage was different from the real, interpersonal contact in the classroom—I just didn't want to replicate the yelling style I had suffered as a child.

I got very depressed about that discovery for a while because, like many people, I like to think that I have conquered my past. I stewed about it until I went through some back articles from a women's studies class I had taken. I found a piece on the power of silence and using silence as a tool. After I read it I realized that I had seen one of my cooperating teachers use silence in his classroom a million times to break the flow of sound and to draw attention to either the material or to whoever was being disruptive in class. I decided to try it and discovered that it not only worked, but it was much more compatible with the way I liked to do things. Then came the tough part—I had to tell my team-teacher about it. I took a deep breath and approached her after class. I told her that I appreciated her point of view and I had tried her approach, but that there was no way I could adopt her method of management because it simply didn't work for me. I also told her that I couldn't make myself become something I wasn't. She stood and stared at me for a minute and then, to my surprise, agreed. One large bridge built in the communication impasse! I feel as though I have a lot more to learn about classroom management, but I determined this semester that under most circumstances, I can hold my own in a classroom.

My final big question going into student teaching was whether or not I really wanted to be a teacher. I asked this one because I had a lot of reasons to doubt my career decision. I knew that I enjoyed the students, but I was very uncertain whether or not I could handle the pressures of teaching. Right away in the semester I decided I couldn't. I spent the first three weeks of my time as a student teacher in shell shock. Not only was I reliving my own painful school experiences right and left, but I had a terrible time drawing boundaries between myself and the students I encountered. Because of my tumultuous childhood, I felt almost responsible for each student who came in with emotional or family problems. They were so needy and in some cases desperate for encouragement and support. I felt as thought I had some sort of radar for these students. On top of it all, my own family situation blew up, and my sisters were calling me all the time for help. It seemed like practically everyone around me was some sort of emotional vampire draining their energy from me, and here I was, letting them! After a few weeks when I thought I couldn't stand it any longer, I decided that I had to grow some callouses.

I thought I was doing better until my cooperating teacher and I were grading the students' stories, and we read one by a boy who wrote in graphic detail about being raped by his father. I couldn't finish reading it. I went home and cried for hours, until there was nothing left. I thought that there was no way I could be a teacher if I had to deal with situations like this.

I went to school the next day determined to keep a tighter grip on my emotions. Fortunately, my cooperating teacher had followed up on the story and found out that the boy was getting extensive counseling, so we both felt better. It was a turning point for me. I still felt compassion for the students, but it was comforting to know that there were people to turn to and places to go to get help for these kids.

A lot of other things got me down during the semester too. Dealing with the school bureaucracy was no picnic. (I was amazed at the amount of paperwork the administration required of teachers!) Every self-doubt I ever had in my life popped out to torment me when I was least ready to handle them. My checkbook balance was dangerously low because I had to reduce the hours on my other job to teach. Yet somehow it all seemed to work out all right. I worked hard. I got a lot of encouragement from my cooperating teachers and my team-teacher as well as from other faculty at the school. I got to try some really wild and creative things in the classroom. I enjoyed the students.

I wavered on this final question until just recently. I got a call from a friend of mine, offering me some commercial work, and in addition my office job wanted to increase my work hours. I called another friend and told her about these new possibilities, expecting her to be excited and encouraging. Instead she was silent. I asked her why she seemed so noncommittal, and she replied, "You've never been happier than you have been for these past months. Even when you were crying over some student's behavior or tough life story and swearing that you'd never go back, you were happy somewhere inside because you were learning and they were learning. If you go back to that office, you'll hate it. You have to pursue this teaching thing. If you don't, I honestly have to tell you that I think it would be stupid."

I thought about what she said for a while and agreed. In a backward sort of way these were four of the best months I'd ever had. The constant introspection brought about changes in me that I had never expected. I got to work with some wonderful students and teachers. I finally got to do a job that appealed to me creatively and intellectually. I found strengths in myself that I never knew I had. I also rediscovered how much I enjoy writing and literature.

So, in short, I can now answer my final question—which I really didn't have an answer for until today. I now know what I will be . . . a good, caring teacher.

POINTS TO PONDER

1. In this case, the teacher's philosophy fostered the use of materials that related to the students' lives and involved students in curriculum decisions. What is your philosophy of teaching, and how will these beliefs affect your teaching? Give specific examples. What will you do if your cooperating teacher does not have a similar philosophy?

2. How do you see yourself dealing with the emotional impact of students who have problems that reach beyond the classroom? What resources can you draw on to assist you in situations like this?

3. This teacher wanted to create a sense of community in the classroom. Is this one of your goals? Why or why not? If this is one of your goals, what will you do to try to accomplish it?

4. Think about your style of management in terms of how you will speak to your students to get them back on task or quiet them when necessary.

5. This teacher spoke of dealing with a conflict that occurred with another student teacher. How will you deal with conflict or disagreements that might occur between you and your cooperating teacher? With another teacher in the school?

6. Outside influences may affect your behavior during student teaching. Think about how your own school experience may color your image of what should happen in the classroom. Consider your personal life—how might this place demands on your time? Should you work while student teaching?

7. This student teacher was able to develop lessons without any curriculum constraints. How would you feel about such flexibility? How would you determine what to teach if there were no required curriculum?

 ## FURTHER READING

Bogue, E. G. (1991). *A journey of the heart: The call to teaching.* Bloomington, IN: Phi Delta Kappa Educational Foundation.

Johnson, S. (1991). *Teachers at work: Achieving success in our schools.* New York: Basics Books.

Jones, V., & Jones, L. (1990). *Comprehensive classroom management.* Boston: Allyn & Bacon.

Purkey, W., & Stanley, P. (1991). *Invitational teaching, learning, and living.* Washington, DC: National Education Association.

Schubert, W., & Ayers, W. (Eds.). (1992). *Teacher lore: Learning from our own experience.* New York: Longman.

Strother, D. (Ed.). (1991). *Learning to fail: Case studies of students at risk.* Bloomington, IN: Phi Delta Kappa.

Chapter Six

CONTENT OR KIDS?

SETTING

Sophomore Math Classes

FOCUS QUESTIONS

While reading this case, consider the following questions:

- How important is it to get to know your students?
- What is your responsibility to students beyond teaching the academics?

I was given a choice assignment for student teaching. Besides some regular math classes, I would be teaching a pre-IB (International Baccalaureate) sophomore Geometry class. How did I get so lucky? The IB program is an accelerated course of study in which students take higher level courses throughout high school in pursuit of an IB Diploma. This IB Diploma translates into one year of college coursework. Understandably, most students in these courses are quite motivated. "I won't have to deal with management issues in this class," I thought to myself, "I can really focus on the math!"

My first day teaching went very well. The staff and students were very kind and helpful. I was excited about being a role model for women in math, as the entire Mathematics department was male. All of my students seemed to like me right away. All of them except Tammy, that is. Even thought she was in my pre-IB class, she made it quite clear that she was not willing to give me a chance. I was told that this was not Tammy's usual behavior, and I wondered why she was so pointedly rude. I had thought the students would enjoy a change of pace. I knew that my style of teaching was similar to my cooperating teacher's, so I thought that having a new teacher would not be too upsetting. Besides, my cooperating teacher and I were really team-teaching at this point in the experience.

Tammy made sarcastic remarks to me every chance she got that first day and every day after that. If I helped other students with their independent practice, Tammy would immediately raise her hand. When I went to assist her, she would yell out, "Well, it's about time! I've had my hand up for at least 10 minutes!" I tried to monitor my involvement with her and looked for her hand as soon as I could, but she seemed to wait until I was working with someone else before she raised her hand. I tried ignoring her. She questioned my comments and answers. Tammy would also frequently announce, "You looked right at me and then went to help Sue (or Tom or Mary) first!" She showed no respect for me at all, and it really began to worry Steve, my cooperating teacher. He told me about a female foreign language teacher in the building who was having a terrible time with Tammy. Tammy spent each period in this woman's class ranting, raving, and swearing at this particular teacher. It was obvious that Tammy had a "you can't make me do anything" attitude.

Steve thought that maybe this attitude problem was connected with gender, that for some reason Tammy did not have respect for female teachers. I set about to find out more about Tammy in an attempt to improve our relationship, even though I was somewhat irked that I had to spend my preparation time (time I really needed to get my lessons ready) doing a background check on this young lady.

I began by speaking to other female teachers to see if they could provide me with any insight into my situation. From them, I found out that Tammy's parents were divorced and that she lived with her mother. Also, Tammy's school performance had been so poor the first semester that she had failed many of her classes. She had a high IQ and had scored very well on her ability test, but had been a better student the year before. Apparently, she had begun hanging around with the tough, smoker crowd and was constantly getting into trouble. In response, her mother had been threatening to send her away to live with her father if her attitude didn't improve. Steve told me that he thought Tammy was seeing the

Wellness Counselor. When I checked into this, I discovered that Tammy had been telling people that she thought it would be cool to die.

I found out more about Tammy than I had anticipated. I had been concerned about getting her to improve her studies in math and her attitude toward me. I had been worried about her respecting me, and now I realized that the situation was much more complicated than that. "Now what am I going to do?" I wondered. "They didn't teach us about this in our teacher prep courses!"

After thinking about this for quite a while, I decided that I would try to pay more attention to Tammy. It seemed to me that she might be using this negative approach to get my attention. Instead of waiting for her hand to go up, I would check in with her first when the students were working independently. I had been trying to ignore her comments, hoping that they would just go away, but I realized that this had not been the best approach. I decided that whenever Tammy had a question, I would answer it. Whenever she made a sarcastic comment, I would just smile and pretend as if it didn't bother me in the least. I would also work through every problem that she requested and show her that I really did know my math!

After I began teaching the class on my own, Tammy was always eager to ask me questions. Most of these questions did not relate to the assignment. She would think of a geometric figure and ask me if it could be constructed in a certain way. I felt as if she was constantly testing me. If I was ever hesitant, her response was, "Well, I guess we'd better go get Mr. Jacobson. I know HE can do this."

In Geometry class, I often allowed students to write out proofs on the board for extra credit coupons. Occasionally the students didn't try to do the proofs as homework, but came to class hoping to just copy them down from someone who was willing to work it at the board. When I ask for volunteers to work the proofs at the board and no one responds, I usually suspect that the homework has not been completed. If the entire class has not tried to work the proofs, I tell them to keep their papers and we will see if anyone has attempted them the next day. I do not believe that they learn how to work the proofs if they simply copy them off of the board. If they need help, I give them hints, but I tell them that they need to develop these sequential problem-solving skills through practice and trial and error. On these problem-proof days, Tammy would always call out, "Aren't you going to do them, Miss Louis? Or can't you?" She tried as hard as she could to upset me and challenge me. Try as she might, I managed to kept my resolve. I was determined to win her over. Day after day I would smile and continue with the lesson.

After a few weeks of my smiling through gritted teeth, Tammy started to change. I thought that maybe I was finally wearing her down with my refusal to respond to her challenges. She became more quiet in class and basically started to ignore me. During this time, she also missed quite a few classes. Class was calmer with her gone, I have to admit. Then one day, she lingered after class by my desk and commented, "I guess I'd better get my grade up in this class."

I asked her why she was interested now after much of the term had passed. I also pointed out that she wasn't failing; she was simply doing mediocre work.

"I'm down to my last chance with my Mom," Tammy stated. "If I don't improve real fast, my Mom is going to send me to live with my Dad. I don't want to go because he lives in a little town where there's nothing to do, and all of my friends are here. Besides he's always at work; I'd just get in the way."

I thought I'd focus on the academic issue and ignore her comments about her Dad. "I know that you have the ability to do better in this class, Tammy," I told her, "but it will take more effort on your part. Why don't you stop in before school if you have some questions about assignments?"

She nodded in agreement and left the room. I watched her go and uttered a sigh of relief. "Maybe this is the breakthrough I hoped for with Tammy. It's the first time she has actually spoken to me without a challenge in her voice—we actually had a personal conversation!" I wondered why this sudden change, why she had trusted me with the information about her Dad. I hoped her grades would improve and she would stop bugging me in class.

As the quarter progressed, Tammy slowly made a turnaround. She began to participate in class in a positive way; the negative and sarcastic remarks became less frequent and then disappeared. She started completing her work and even volunteered to do problems on the board. Because she also seemed to be more pleasant to the other students in the class, group work went more smoothly. Every day, Tammy stopped in before school for extra help. She had usually completed most of her assignment and asked for help with only the tougher problems. She always came to my desk for help, even though Mr. Jacobson was also in the room. I think that she began to believe in my ability to teach math, and even when days didn't go perfectly, the challenges in class were gone. Tammy was friendly and funny in class and seemed so much happier with herself and with me. I was amazed at this turnaround and reluctant to believe that I had anything to do with it.

When Steve and I were reflecting on Tammy today and all of the problems that we had anticipated, we were both amazed that things were going so well. Tammy asked me the other day how much longer I would be teaching her class. When I told her that May 13 was my last day, she was really unhappy. She said, "You can't leave! We'll be lost without you!" This statement surprised me; Tammy was not a student I had expected to reach.

When I asked the students in my classes to complete an evaluation of my teaching, I wondered what Tammy's would say. When I read her evaluation, a statement surprised me. She said that at first I seemed only concerned with the right answer and the bright kids. She said that most teachers expected her to do poorly because she hung around with people who weren't the "goody two-shoes," but that I had told her that I thought she was capable of doing the work. Had that one statement made such a difference?

I came to my student teaching experience expecting to teach math, but it seemed that the interactions between Tammy and me had been about more than just the subject. Although I was initially irritated that I had to do more that just teach math, the time I took to understand Tammy and deal with her behavior paid off. I don't know if this approach will work in every situation, but I certainly believe that, as a teacher, I have an obligation to try to understand the needs of every student. I just wonder what I will do when I *can't* reach someone. Is it fair to the other kids in a class when one (or two) kids are disruptive? How long could I maintain my grin-and-bear-it attitude? When do we give up on kids like Tammy if they don't seem to want to succeed?

POINTS TO PONDER

1. What do you think was the cause the struggle between Tammy and this student teacher? Do you think this is a common occurrence? What do you think are your responsibilities to students who behave like Tammy? What are your responsibilities to the rest of the class?

2. What is your primary responsibility in the classroom? Do you have the time and expertise to deal with student problems that are unrelated to the coursework?

3. What are your expectations for the classes you might be teaching during student teaching? Do you think preconceived ideas about students and particular classes can affect your work in the classroom?

4. What assistance from the cooperating teacher might you expect in a situation like this? What do you think about Tammy's cooperating teacher's response? What additional resources are available to assist you with a student like this?

5. How do you think other students reacted to this teacher's attention to Tammy? Do you think the student teacher's response was fair to everyone?

6. What approach might you have taken initially in dealing with the comments Tammy was making in class?

7. Do you think that this conflict could have escalated into a power struggle between Tammy and the student teacher? What are other examples of power struggles in the classroom, and how will you deal with this issue?

FURTHER READING

Beane, J. A., & Lipka, R. (1987). *When the kids come first: Enhancing self-esteem.* Columbus, OH: National Middle School Association.

Glasser, W. (1992) *The quality school: Managing students without coercion.* New York: Harper Collins Publishers.

Gregory, T. B., & Smith, G. R. (1987). *High schools as communities: The small school reconsidered.* Bloomington, IN: Phi Delta Kappa Educational Foundation.

Kohn, A. (1994, December). The truth about self-esteem. *Phi Delta Kappan, 76*(4), 273–283.

Prokop, M. S. (1990). Children of divorce: Relearning happiness. *Momentum, 21*(2), 72–73.

Chapter Seven

TIME PRESSURES

SETTING

Sixth Grade

FOCUS QUESTIONS

While reading this case, consider the following questions:

- How do you utilize time effectively in the classroom?
- What is your classroom management plan?

The kind of teacher I seemed to be at the conclusion of my student teaching experience was not how I had imagined myself to be prior to this experience. Having realized during my education classes that traditional techniques tend to lead to simple memorization without understanding, I knew I wanted to use inquiry techniques and hands-on activities as my main teaching methods. I had imagined class time to be spent with projects and discussion, and I assumed that this would require some amount of freedom and trust for the students. Quite simply, I hoped for a democratic classroom. I should add that I was not oblivious to the intricacies of children's behavior and thoughts, yet I believed I could whirl my students into my own excitement about learning and the subjects, especially my second major, Mathematics.

My excitement increased as I learned in the first days of observation that my assignment was exactly the one for which I had hoped. The school was in the city and had a multicultural base, and yet its accomplishments rose far above its reputation as an inner city school. My cooperating teacher made it obvious that he was going to give me a great deal of freedom and an equal amount of support. I believed that I had everything I needed to become the teacher I imagined myself to be. However, things did not proceed as planned. My sixth graders, grouped for math and switched with another teacher so that I taught three math classes, provided different sets of troubles.

The first group that I took over was a lower level group that focused on math basics. The ages and abilities of the children were wide ranging. I was told that these kids had gotten mostly unsatisfactory grades during fifth-grade math (and maybe fourth grade as well) because of language barriers, laziness, slight learning disabilities, and lack of understanding of mathematics. Yet I felt I could handle these problems. There was help for the ESL students, there were practical life applications I could implement for laziness, and tutoring was available for those with difficulties learning math. Yet one hurdle was so high that I felt powerless to jump it: THE CLOCK. This math group met first thing in the morning, and after a long bus ride to provide integration in the school, the children were still sleepy. In addition, I would often face a half-empty (or should I say half-full) classroom. I saw some students only once or twice a week, and others less than that. I wasn't sure what I should do about this problem. Was I supposed to call parents and ask why their kids missed school so often? Most of the kids returned with an "excused" absence. Perhaps a new policy for absenteeism might work for some students, although I had no idea what that policy should be (and I was fearful of criticizing the administration for what I thought was a lack of efficiency). There were also an unbelievable number of classes that were "cancelled" for movies, speakers, or some other event. I looked at the curriculum I was supposed to cover and knew we would never get there. I wondered if "coverage" was really that important. Wouldn't mastery of some skills be more vital than simply "getting through" the curriculum? How did I really know if the kids had learned anything? Did presenting the material really equate with teaching? In the meantime, keeping track of the learning for all the students whom I didn't know—some of whom I would never know—seemed nearly impossible and far too time-consuming.

Still, this class held many joys for me. I watched students who barely understood English learn math with designated partners. I tutored students who thought they could never understand math and saw them get excited when they realized what multiplication and division were all about. The students also made some connections between life and math as we figured out which items purchased at stores were the best buy or determined how much was saved when an item was marked 25% off. Yet I believe I let so many students go because I felt too overwhelmed with policy. Instead of tackling the problem—working with my cooperating teacher or the administration to deal with the absenteeism—I felt there was nothing I could do. So I did very little.

As my student teaching continued, I began teaching the additional math group as well as language arts, science, and social studies. This experience started and ended very differently, again because of time constraints. I couldn't seem to keep my new students on task because of one simple concept: classroom management. The math group started off very talkative while silence reigned during the other subjects. This trend soon reversed itself. Because I wanted to have a democratic classroom, I tried to achieve this as quickly as possible. I gave many freedoms, and once I loosened control, I lost it. As the students seemed to erupt into chaos or ignore my questions with uninterested silence, I lost my self-esteem and began to question my ability as a teacher.

Class time became a time for struggling and "shushing," and as a result, I lost faith in my ability to have projects and hands-on activities. Day after day I turned to worksheets and "teacher talk" to plow through the material, hoping that my assignment sheets and quizzes were keeping students on their toes. Opportunities to praise students for thoughtful questions and answers passed by more times than I could count as we continued to drill and complete worksheets that I generated night after night. My continuous talking drained my students' creativity as well as my own. Every day, I left the classroom more tired than the day before.

So, here I am, six months later, having just accepted my first teaching position. Did I find answers to all my concerns during my student teaching experience? Yes and no. After months of reflection, I have realized that no one was more critical of my teaching ability during student teaching than I was. I had great support during student teaching, yet I all but ignored praise because I was not the teacher I imagined myself to be. I was quick to listen to criticism but quicker to ignore a pat on the back. There were great days when I left school feeling I had picked the perfect career. Yet, I took the many hard days and let them drain my self-esteem and creativity so much that at times I dreaded the next day. My cooperating teacher tried to reassure me that the kids were learning, but the classroom seemed to be a dull shadow of what I had envisioned. I am sure the students were quick to pick up on my daily loss of energy and enthusiasm.

I now believe that maximizing time on task in the classroom is important, but that it can be achieved only with assistance. Teachers should spend time wisely in the classroom. All new teachers have three important tools that they should not be afraid to use in structuring class time more effectively: management, administration, and parents.

● **Management:** If I had thought out my approach to the classroom and established rules for the mutual development of our democratic classroom, I would not have been unglued by the students' response to more freedom. A democratic classroom still needs guidelines and a disciplined approach. Too much time is lost when teachers don't communicate expectations clearly. New teachers need a discipline policy that is completely thought out, and they must be willing to follow through on it. I'm not saying that I won't be flexible, but next time I will provide a model for classroom behavior before attempting total classroom democracy.

● **Administration:** The administration is there to back up teachers, and the administration in my school was particularly strong and supportive. I did not take advantage of their help because I thought it might make me look weak to have to go to the principal. It is reasonable to expect administration to assist with issues that affect learning time. The need for a clear and enforced tardy policy as well as support for dealing with truant children is something that should be discussed with the administration. In the future, I will take my concerns to the administration and be willing help work for change in policy, if necessary.

● **Parents:** I will make an effort to call parents more often in my new position. Even if parents do not respond, I need to try. Classroom newsletters sent home can help. It is important to send positive notes, too, not just notes to parents about problems! I found that when I did connect with parents (often because they came to me), they were usually supportive and wanted to help their child succeed. I need to work on connecting school and home for these children and let parents know that I want their children to be in school.

I still think that active learning is the most effective approach to dealing with children, but I now recognize that each day—bad or good—is a learning experience. I can't give up if something is difficult. I need to modify and adjust my lessons, and I have to be ready with relevant examples and prepared activities for all subject areas. I am a new teacher and, as a result, a learner. I need to go in with the basics and work toward my goal. All of this takes time; I do not have the years of experience that my cooperating teacher has, but I can gain it—year by year! I know that time can be a resource that works for you or against you. With time and effort, I will someday (not tomorrow and not this first year—but someday) be the teacher I know I can be.

POINTS TO PONDER

1. What situations in this student teaching experience created difficulties for this teacher?

2. This teacher identified some "joys" that occurred with her first math group. What do you think of her teaching strategies? What teaching methods would you employ in this situation?

3. This teacher speaks of a need for a management plan. Have you defined your method of dealing with behavior problems when you are teaching? Be specific.

4. Discuss the implications of time in the classroom. How can you improve time on task when students are not in school? Whose problem is this?

5. How would you evaluate this student teacher based on this case? What did the teacher do well? What suggestions might you have that would have improved the situation?

6. What do you think about the three tools this teacher mentions: management, administration, and parents? How will you use these tools?

FURTHER READING

Doyle, W., & Carter, K. (1987), Choosing the means of instruction. In V. Richardson-Koehler (Ed.), *Educator's handbook: A research perspective* (pp. 188–206). White Plains, NY: Longman.

Swap, S. A. (1993). *Developing home-school partnerships: From concepts to practice.* New York: Teachers College Press.

Walberg, H. (1988, March). Synthesis of research on time and learning. *Educational Leadership*, 76–80+.

Weinstein, C. S., & Mignano, A. J. (1993). *Elementary classroom management: Lessons from research and practice.* New York: McGraw-Hill.

Chapter Eight

IS HONESTY THE BEST POLICY?

SETTING

Senior Math Class

FOCUS QUESTIONS

While reading this case, consider the following questions:

- How do we determine what students know?
- What is the purpose of assessment?

The most vivid memory from my student teaching is an incident of cheating in my senior honors math class. I gave the students a take-home test with only one rule: They had to work by themselves. They could use any resource but each other. I gave them the test and sent them off to complete it, confident that these intelligent young people would use their additional time wisely. Several days later I collected the tests. In the grading process I noticed one huge red flag, an addition mistake that almost one third of the class seemed to make. Taking a closer look, the signs of cheating were obvious. After talking to my cooperating teacher, I decided I would let the students decide their own fate. I would give them an F (50%), which wouldn't totally destroy their grade for the course if they admitted to the cheating. However, their final grade was determined by an average of their test scores. I told them that I would give them a zero if they didn't own up to their dishonesty. I was firm, and they knew that I was aware of what had occurred. I heard several pleas of guilty after class.

The big problem was Kathy. She was one of my favorite students—a hard worker, a very good student. Her paper also contained that same mistake that had alerted me to the other students' cheating. She did not, however, admit to collaboration with the others. I called her in to talk about it after school. She claimed that she had changed that one particular answer just before handing it in. She said that she had spent hours of her own time on this exam and pointed out that her work showed it. She had just made one dumb mistake before class. (She had actually changed her correct answer to an incorrect one under pressure from seeing her peers' different response.) She went on to say that everyone had cheated, that many different groups were involved, and that those who were not caught had just been more subtle. She gave me the names of those she claimed had also cheated. I told her that I could prove the cheating I'd identified because they had all made the same mistake, and that it was highly unlikely that this was a random occurrence. I told her that there was no evidence of her claim that others had also cheated. I said that I had to be consistent and that I could respond only to the facts as I knew them. She broke down and cried and left the room.

This incident was hard on me. I was upset that cheating had occurred and that she had been a part of it. As a result, an individual whom I had considered one of my top students, someone I enjoyed working with in the classroom, was obviously very angry. Our relationship changed in that instant and never went back to the way it was before. This incident, which I had tried to handle so carefully, had taken a very unexpected turn.

Kathy wasn't the only one who was upset. Her parents were angry as well. Kathy was concerned about getting into college and competing for scholarships. A low grade in a key math class could ruin her chances for success. Her parents called the principal, and the principal talked to my cooperating teacher, who talked to me. The fact that Kathy also had cystic fibrosis was brought up, a fact that I had been previously unaware of. I was told that the administration would like me to change my decision, to come up with some alternative. My cooperating teacher said that he would support me regardless of my decision, but that it might be a difficult situation if I persisted.

I believe that students need to learn to be honest and that cheating has consequences. I trusted these kids and expected them to respond honestly in a situation in which I had given them an opportunity to lessen the pressure by giving a take-home exam. They had the chance to do well on the test by taking it home and using resources not available to them in the classroom. Life doesn't always give second chances, but I gave one to my students. I offered an in-class retake test for any student who wanted to take it. They all did.

This incident was difficult for me and for the students. I learned that competition for grades is greater than I had expected. I hope they learned something about honesty. I know I learned that at times teachers have to back down from their initial stance. I know what it is like to lose your rapport with a class and to lose your trust in what they can do.

Did I ask too much? Were my expectations too great? I will definitely rethink the parameters for giving a take-home test. I will let my students know what my feelings are regarding dishonesty. But if faced with an obvious and outright incident of cheating, I intend to enforce the consequences I have established. I think students should pay the penalty—they need to learn that life doesn't give second chances.

◎ POINTS TO PONDER

1. Is competition in the classroom a good thing? Why or why not? Should you encourage or discourage competition? What forms of assessment might counteract students' concerns about grades, which often fuel competition?

2. What are other options for assessment that might be appropriate in this situation? Can collaborative exams be worthwhile examples of student learning?

3. What are your views of ethics in the classroom? Is honesty a value that can be taught to students? If so, how would you integrate this into your curriculum? At what grade level should cheating be punished? What kinds of consequences should be enforced?

4. Does the student teacher seem to need to be the authority on this matter? Does he seem open to students' and parents' perspectives?

5. What should the role of the administration be in decisions made by teachers? What involvement will the administrator(s) at your student teaching site have in your experience?

6. How will you deal with disgruntled parents? What resources are available to help you communicate effectively with parents?

FURTHER READING

Ackerman, P. (1971). The effect of honor grading on students' test scores. *American Educational Research Journal, 8*(2), 321–333.

Curwin, R. (1992). *Rediscovering hope: Our greatest teaching strategy.* Bloomington, IN: National Educational Service.

Gathercoal, F. (1993). *Judicious discipline.* San Francisco: Caddo Gap Press.

Mendler, A. (1992). *What do I do when . . . ? How to achieve discipline with dignity in the classroom.* Bloomington, IN: National Educational Service.

Maeroff, G. (1991). Assessing alternative assessment. *Phi Delta Kappan, 73,* 272–281.

Wolf, D., Bixby, J., Glenn, J., III, & Gardner, H. (1991). To use their minds well: New forms of student assessment. *Review of Research in Education, 17,* 31–74.

Chapter Nine

KEEPING MY COOL: CLASSROOM MANAGEMENT

SETTING

Second Grade

FOCUS QUESTIONS

When reading this case, consider the following questions:

- What is your management plan for your classroom?
- How will you assimilate your plan into the management plan of your cooperating teacher?

I began my student teaching experience in Lois Kemp's second grade in an urban school with a very diverse population. I entered school green and idealistic. When I left 15 weeks later, I was definitely more grounded. I realized that my earlier perceptions about teaching and the reality of the classroom weren't mutually exclusive, but darn close.

I walked into Central Elementary the first day defined as a student teacher: all student, no teacher. I had an idea of what teaching was all about. My philosophy espoused a setting where I presented material, the students were on task 100% of the time, the class virtually ran itself, and everyone learned all that I had to teach. Obviously this is a somewhat simplified version of my total educational philosophy, but from a student's perspective (which I had developed for 21 years of my life) teaching looked easy and appeared to involve very little work. Wrong! Sitting in a college classroom for four years learning how to educate students in no way compares to the knowledge gained from the realities of teaching. Oh, I'd had my share of field experiences. I had even taught lessons. But those isolated experiences didn't capture the realities of the day-to-day existence in the classroom.

The dynamics of the classroom and the responsibilities I had overwhelmed me at first. What got to me were the little things that I hadn't thought about and experienced before, such as taking attendance when all these little people were busy sharpening pencils and chatting with their friends. Who was where?

Getting students to be quiet was a challenge to my patience . . . and encouraging students to pay attention and be on task shaped my first few days:

"It's time to sit down and get to work."

"Please tone it down class."

"Yes, you need to draw a line from the word to the picture."

"All right, you can leave for your Chapter I class."

"Didn't you realize you would need your pencil for class?"

"Here's your pass to go to the bathroom."

"ERIC! PLEASE BE QUIET! I'm NOT going to tell you again!"

"Everyone needs to come sit down in the story circle. I said IN the circle, not under the table."

"Are we all listening?"

"Please push your chairs in."

"Don't forget to put on your boots!"

"HAVE A NICE EVENING!"

These were typical pieces of dialogue from my first lessons. I handled the stressful situations better as I got to know the children. It was easier to direct a child when I didn't have to say, "You there . . . " Of course, I quickly learned the names of the children who were consistently off task; I struggled with those who were quiet and cooperative. As I grew to know the active children, I began to see their energy as a positive force to channel into learning rather than something to curtail. I began to relax, and I found that my level of tolerance grew. Learning is noisy, and memories of my classmates and I sitting in rapt attention during elementary school are obviously from another era. These children were fun and endearing, but they often really needed to move around and talk.

My cooperating teacher was a wonderful role model. It is amazing she didn't pull out her hair and send me packing those first days when I taught. She reminded me that the children came from environments that were different from what I had experienced and that expecting silence in a classroom didn't support the learning style of most of the students in my room. I knew all of these things from a course I had had in multiculturalism in college, but textbook knowledge didn't dissolve my initial discomfort with what I perceived as disorder.

Eventually the students began to respond to me, to see me as the teacher. We became comfortable with each other. After some time, Racine began to bring a pencil to class. Marty stopped running everywhere, and Shana didn't always ask me to repeat directions five or six times. The reason for these and other successes was the gradual transition that occurred in my class—from chaotic teaching situations to a controlled and cooperative learning environment. This was accomplished by changing my educational philosophy and classroom management techniques.

For some reason, all of the discussions we'd had in our methods classes in college flew out of my mind when I faced this energetic group of second graders. Lois used groups in most of her lessons, and I knew the elements of cooperative learning: individual accountability, positive interdependence, face-to-face interaction, and all of that. But when the room got noisy with the sounds of 26 children, I had a tough time. That old adage "I couldn't hear myself think" came to mind, and I certainly needed to think about what I was doing when teaching a lesson. Still, I began to see that classroom management was a part of the plan for learning and that the two could not be separated or isolated.

How did my transformation occur? Lois and my college supervisor were wonderful. They never gave up on me but encouraged me and worked with me until I was successful. We did a lot of team-teaching, and I learned that my focus on discipline was getting in the way. Lois talked about her classroom management plan, which emphasized a positive learning environment for students without placing total concentration on difficulties AFTER they arise. Her focus was on planning well and being proactive about what was acceptable behavior in the classroom. She had involved the children in setting the standards earlier in the year. I failed to follow through on the consequences, and the children ran right over me.

One basic tool that I didn't use at first was the makeup of the groups. The children sat at tables of four, and they worked together for approximately six weeks. This close proximity encouraged talking, but I didn't feel comfortable enforcing the rule and moving anyone to the "solo station" when the talking got out of hand. The children had established this rule about respecting the person speaking (teacher or student) and the subsequent consequence, but my lack of familiarity with the process, and my focus on teaching the content, made me forget the procedures. I thought if I just talked louder I would be able to get the students' attention. Unfortunately, I do not have a booming voice, and I left after my first week of teaching with a hoarse voice and raw throat. Telling students to be quiet would work for a brief period before the noise would return to its previous level. I would tell the students repeatedly to quiet down—but to no avail.

My cooperating teacher suggested that I use silence and wait-time to let the students know that it was time to quiet down. We had talked about this is education classes also, but again, in the I tended to jump right in with admonitions rather than waiting. My silence seemed to me a mark of my inefficiency, and waiting a few seconds seemed like an eternity. Lois showed me how she would stop, step back, and look up, waiting for the students to notice her irritation. The students would quickly shush each other, and after thanking them for their cooperation, Lois would continue. The class did not move on until the students complied. After a few weak starts, I managed to wait rather than tell the students to be quiet or just talk over them. Gradually, I began to use this tool efficiently and comfortably.

I also rediscovered that the students were much more intent on learning if they were active participants. My concern over the loud and active behavior had initially lead me to try to squelch the children's natural tendency to "do" rather than listen. We used manipulatives for math, and I brought in candy bars (three per table) that each group had to divide into four equal portions. Having the students do hands-on work with materials made the class noisier, but quite productive. By allowing and encouraging students to work together with direction and guidance from me, we had some amazing lessons. When a student became too excited and forgot our class rules, the use of wait-time and a reminder usually worked. In some situations time at the "solo station" was required. When the time came to regroup the children, I used observations that Lois and I had made to place children at tables where they would be comfortable, where they could learn from other members in the group, and where they would be less likely to be off-task. This was very effective. I also found that I was keeping my distance from the children and planting myself at the front of the classroom. Again, Lois modeled her movement around the classroom, and her willingness to stoop down and talk to the children eye-to-eye, at their level. The effectiveness of standing near a child who was not on-task or briefly sitting at a table to help the group with their work was impressive, and I began to find it comfortable to roam the room.

The main thing I have learned from this experience is that teaching is a dynamic process comprised of many variables that I, as the teacher, must continually monitor and adjust to achieve my objectives. It is hard work, requiring lots of patience. You can't just react—you have to be thoughtful in your response. Lois and her class had developed class rules, but I had initially felt those rules were for the kids. By failing to follow through on the consequences that had been established prior to my arrival, I created a situation where the students were often off-task.

My nervousness and desire to be a "good" teacher almost prevented me from being successful in this experience. I have learned a lot. I realize now that teaching is more than disseminating information to students. It is a job in which I am in charge of directing a classroom of students who are engaged in their own learning. Facilitating rather than preaching; providing structure, guidance, and support—these are the tasks of the successful classroom teacher. It is my responsibility to provide a safe learning environment in which everyone can succeed and each individual student need is met. This means I will have to continually learn new methods for dealing with the unique problems and personalities I will encounter in my classroom. It is important that the students learn not only the subject matter, but also how to be responsible for themselves, and that can occur only when I involve them in the learning. New situations are always difficult, but I know I can control students' behavior in the classroom, because I will be proactive in planning my classroom management approach.

◉ POINTS TO PONDER

1. Share your management plan with your peers. What adjustments would you be willing to make if this plan doesn't prove to be effective?

2. Consider the initial comments made by this student teacher in the dialogue included in the text. What else could the teacher have said or done?

3. What is your image of an effective classroom? Do you expect students to be quiet during lessons?

4. How does learning style affect the conversation in the classroom and classroom behavior?

5. Describe how cooperative learning methods can assist with classroom management.

◉ FURTHER READING

Cazden, C. (1988). *Classroom discourse: The language of teaching and learning.* Portsmouth, NH: Heinemann.

Ivey, A., & Gluckstern, N. (1982). *Basic attending skills* (2nd ed.). North Amherst, MA: Microtraining Associates.

Ivey, A., & Gluckstern, N. (1984). *Basic influencing skills* (2nd ed.). North Amherst, MA: Microtraining Associates.

Jones, V., & Jones, L. (1990). *Comprehensive classroom management: Motivating and managing students* (3rd ed.). Boston: Allyn & Bacon.

Slavin, R. (1991). Synthesis of research on cooperative learning. *Educational Leadership, 48*(5), 71–82.

Weinstein, C., & Mignano, A. (1993). *Elementary classroom management.* New York: McGraw-Hill, Inc.

Chapter Ten

INCLUSION CONCLUSIONS

SETTING

Ninth-Grade English

FOCUS QUESTIONS

While reading this case, consider the following questions:

- What are the classroom teacher's responsibilities regarding special education students?

- Where do you expect to find the curriculum that you will teach? Should the text be the curriculum?

- How will you plan to meet the different ability levels within your classroom?

When I walked into my ninth-grade assignment for student teaching at a suburban junior high school, I envisioned myself as someone who would inspire my students to engage in discussions of great literary works and compose clear papers. This was a required English course that was to prepare students for the world of high school the following year, and I was excited about the challenge ahead. What I didn't expect to face were the issues raised by inclusion. I figured I was here to learn to teach English and that someone else would handle the special ed students. I had learned about mainstreaming in my education courses, but that was not my primary focus. I believed that I would be able focus my efforts on generating one good lesson for each class that would be workable for all my students. This was not the case.

In my first class I met Steve, who was deaf. He had an interpreter who came with him to class. They communicated in sign language, and the interpreter translated everything the teacher said. This was disturbing. I had envisioned lively discussion among my students; having to wait for someone to interpret what everyone said would certainly put a crimp in my free-flowing style of teaching.

The second class that I would eventually be fully responsible for included six EBD (Emotional/Behavioral Disorder) students. Due to the scheduling of their resource classes, they had all ended up in this one English course. When my cooperating teacher identified them as EBD students, I flashed back to the readings I had been required to digest in my coursework that detailed the wide range of possible reasons for this classification. I wondered how the first unit I had been assigned to teach, on *A Tale of Two Cities,* would go over with this crowd!

The first few days I observed the classes and noticed that Steve would usually read on his own during class, regardless of what the teacher was doing. No one asked him to put down the book. He and his interpreter would often hold conversations in sign language. When I asked about this, my teacher said that this was how she modified her teaching for him—he worked on his own, reading course materials as well as books that he selected. She said that Steve was very bright. With his interpreter's help, he wrote reports on what he read and submitted these for a grade. I thought about what I had heard regarding the purpose of mainstreaming: to include the students in an environment where they could interact with students who did not have a disability. It didn't seem to me that Steve was connecting with anyone in that room. I began to wonder about whether all students could, or should, be doing the same work in this class.

The group of EBD students all sat together in the back of the room. A resource teacher from the Special Education department came in several days a week to pull these kids out into the hall to work with them and catch them up on the reading, to enable them to do the work that everyone else in the class was completing. I wondered how they felt being identified as kids who needed extra help. I was advised by my cooperating teacher that I would need to be tough on these kids, that they could be lazy at times and had to be held accountable for their lessons. Watching their uninterested and bored looks, it seemed to me that they did not want to be in school, and they certainly didn't seem too excited about our upcoming unit on *A Tale of Two Cities.*

When I finally began to teach, I started out with my lesson the way I had envisioned it—laying the background for the novel, assigning reading, and facilitating follow-up discussions. I was pleased with the response of most of the students, but Steve and the EBD crew were obviously not an active part of what was going on in class. I tried all of my "effective questioning" ideas from methods class, but after a week of struggling with this nonparticipation, I took my cooperating teacher's suggestion and sought out the Special Education office to get some new ideas.

Sharon, the lead special education teacher, was wonderful. We set a time to talk after school, and she helped me generate a plan of action. I wanted these students to discuss the readings with everyone else, and I asked Sharon how I could accomplish this. I had called on all of these kids, trying to give them clues to the answer I was looking for, but was met with shrugs and "I don't know" from the EBD group and indifferent silence from Steve. Sharon assured me that there was no reason the students couldn't meet the objective of discussing the literature. She said that there could be more effective modifications than a "pull out remediation plan" or "working independently" IF I was able to spend a little more time and effort. After facing those blank faces the week before, I knew that I wanted more for these kids.

Reading the students' files and talking with their resource teachers and Sharon helped me understand the students' backgrounds more completely. As I read their school histories, the students became more than just the mainstreamed kids. I wondered if I should have looked over these files before I began teaching. It was apparent that Steve was very intelligent. Because he seemed reluctant to participate in our large class discussion, and considering that he did not interact with the rest of the class, I decided it was time to implement some cooperative learning strategies. I thought that this might also help break up the group at the back of the room and engage the EBD students with the rest of the class. Sharon agreed and offered her encouragement.

Instead of my orchestrated whole-class discussion, the next day I put students into groups, assigned roles, and gave them some discussion questions to answer. One student in Steve's group complained to me, saying "He can't talk!" Before I could respond, Steve signed, and his interpreter replied, "I can talk—just not with words." After a few moments of silence, his group got busy and completed their questions.

As time went on and I rotated group roles, I found that Steve was an effective leader. He had already read the novel, and he provided some interesting insights for his group. It seemed to me that Steve had never been asked to put down his book and join the class. The cooperative learning approach, in which everyone is accountable for a specific task yet all receive one grade for the completion of the day's assignment, forced him to be accountable. And as a by-product, the students began to interact with him.

I asked Steve after class one day if he would teach me some of his signs, and I was amazed by the complexity of his language. There was a sign for every word! I thought about having him teach the whole class some signs but decided to wait until both he and the class were more comfortable together. (I might do this earlier the next time.) I talked to Sharon about it, and she said to ask Steve. She mentioned that many times we make decisions for students with disabilities without asking their opinion. She asked whether I would make a decision like this without asking someone who did not have a hearing impairment. She had a point, but I didn't want to put Steve on the spot. I worried that the class might ridicule him. Things had been going pretty smoothly, and I didn't want to take the chance, so I nixed the idea.

Our next unit was on poetry, and one of my objectives was to get students to listen to and appreciate the sound of spoken poetry. To have the students demonstrate that they had met this objective, I included an oral presentation/report as a final grade. Students had to research a poet and give a brief oral presentation about his or her life and work, which included the reading of at least one poem. I worried about Steve. Some of the teachers I talked to in the lounge said that he couldn't do this assignment, that I would really be grading the interpreter as she spoke. I was asked how I would grade Steve, compared to other students. Sharon suggested that I avoid comparing Steve to the other students, but that I set up some criteria that focused on content and could be met via any "language." I made a checklist that broke the components of the assignments into parts, and the criteria of "reading the poem with inflection" and "using correct phrasing while reading the poem to ensure the meaning is conveyed" were the only two that I considered would be hard for Steve to complete himself. Still, he could do the other parts of the assignment—the research and organization of the presentation—so I knew that he could get a passing grade.

As it turned out, Steve's presentation was fantastic! The students in this class had never seen him give a formal presentation, but with his interpreter standing to the side, he gave us some facts and then used the nonverbal expressiveness of his language to "recite" the poem. Both the students and I were impressed. Our last unit, on reading and writing autobiographies, also went well, and Steve didn't hide behind his book. And if he started reading and shutting us out, he always put the book down when I asked him to.

While this plan worked well for Steve, I was worried that I might not get as much involvement from the EBD students. As their reading levels were significantly lower than the majority of the class, the resource teacher had been reading to the students and asking them about the assignments during their "pull out" hallway sessions. With Sharon's approval, I devised a plan in which I identified the key sections of each chapter of our upcoming novel and had these students read only those sections. By generating this modified reading list and individually encouraging each student to complete them for the next class, we cut out the hallway sessions. This way, the students could participate in our cooperative lessons. Carol, the resource teacher, rotated from group to group as the students interacted and offered assistance and suggestions.

While it seemed to me that these students didn't like the traditional classroom structure, my cooperating teacher thought I was giving them too much freedom with my cooperative approach. In addition, the modifications did take more time. On top of what I was doing to prepare for the lesson as a whole, I had to generate the activities and questions for our cooperative groups as well as identify the sections for the EBD group to read. It had been easier when I ran the show, leading discussions from my notes and lecturing in between. I guess I was trying to have the class fit the student's needs a bit more, although *A Tale of Two Cities* probably wouldn't be my first choice of material. After I had been using these various methods for a few weeks, I found that I was more relaxed and enjoyed teaching more. Still, things didn't always go smoothly. One day one of my EBD students kicked over a desk and yelled the "F" word when his group challenged his comments on a question. I had to have him leave the room with Carol and go down to the resource room to cool off.

I tried to talk to all my students informally before and after class or in the cafeteria at lunch sometimes. I wanted to get to know them on a personal level, and this seemed especially important with Jim, Tony, Sarah, Mike, Larry, and Rob—the EBD crowd. Because these students had a reputation for being a tough crowd, many teachers responded by becoming very authoritarian with them. After a few weeks of personal contact, I gained some level of trust with these students that hadn't been there before, and this enabled me to get them to participate more in class. I wanted to allow them to be successful, and this really fell into place when we got to the autobiography unit. These kids had stories to tell, and they wanted to be heard. With encouragement, they produced some wonderful autobiographies. The spelling wasn't accurate, sentences weren't always complete, and they were shorter than many of the other papers, but they powerfully told their own stories. These students were participating at a level appropriate for them—and this was how I had envisioned mainstreaming.

By the end of my student teaching experience, I felt that I was ready to teach English, but I also realized that not all of my students would be enthused about what we read, and not all of their papers would be perfect. I really need to be able to differentiate my instruction based on the needs and abilities of my students. This was a far cry from my original image of myself in the classroom! I also had a lot of questions left to be answered. I wondered if I would be able to choose material that might excite students about learning more than the curriculum I had been given to teach. I wondered how rigidly I needed to comply with district curriculum guidelines. And how would I ever prepare for classes if I was constantly searching out new material? Still, this experience did show me that I could, with support from resource teachers and other colleagues, bring every student to a higher level of knowledge than they were when they started the class. For me, that is what teaching is all about. I know I see my role in the classroom a bit differently than my peers who had few, if any, mainstreamed students in their classes. My goal is not just to teach English, but to teach all young people that they can be successful. English class is the place where, together, we can make that happen.

POINTS TO PONDER

1. How do you envision yourself in a classroom? Does this vision include effective interactions with mainstreamed students? Or do you typically see yourself in a classroom filled with traditional, success-oriented students? What is the reality of classrooms today?

2. How can you create reasonable accommodations for students with disabilities so that they can be successful in your class? What changes must be made in terms of grading? Must all students meet the same goals? What resources are available for you to help with these decisions? How will you meet the needs of the gifted as well as the needs of those who are identified as special education students in your classroom?

3. Discuss how you would implement a cooperative learning approach to your classroom? What do you think is needed for cooperative learning to be successful? What impact would this have on your teaching? Would this shift your role as teacher in the classroom?

4. Curriculum materials are often predetermined before you student teach. Consider some texts or traditional units of study that might be used in your field or for the age group you plan to teach. Will these prescribed materials be your curriculum? In what ways could you supplement existing materials to generate lessons that engage students at a more personal level?

5. What can you do when you are a classroom teacher to improve or affect the selection of curricular materials? How will you respond if you are hired by a district that uses materials or curriculum that you are unfamiliar with or that you feel is inappropriate or outdated?

6. This student teacher dealt with some difficult behaviors in the classroom. How would you react to similar situations—in particular if students use profanity in the classroom or react violently? Does your classroom management style need to be adjusted when dealing with special needs students? What more do you feel you need to learn about special needs students?

 ## FURTHER READING

Choate, J. S. (1993). *Successful mainstreaming: Proven ways to detect and correct special needs.* Boston: Allyn & Bacon.

Duke, D. L., & Meckel, A. M. (1984). *Teacher's guide to classroom management.* New York: Random House.

Rottier, J., & Ogan, B. (1991). *Cooperative learning in middle-level schools.* Washington, DC: National Education Association.

Slavin, R. (1991). *Student team learning: A practical guide to cooperative learning.* Washington, DC: National Education Association.

Zirpoli, T., & Melloy, K. (1993). *Behavior management: Applications for teachers and parents.* Upper Saddle River, NJ: Merrill/Prentice Hall.

Part Two

TWICE-TOLD TALES

*Experiences from the perspective
of a college supervisor . . .*

Chapter Eleven

LOOKING IN THE MIRROR

SETTING

First Grade

FOCUS QUESTIONS

While reading this case, consider the following questions:

- How can you maximize your learning and development during your student teaching experience?
- What tools are available to provide you with information regarding your teaching performance?

I first observed Cheri during the morning of her second day as a student teacher in Joan Robinson's class. Energetic and eager, I knew that Cheri was well organized and knowledgeable from my interaction with her during in my college classes. The first-grade students were in their second semester of school and were well acclimated to the classroom routine. Cheri took attendance while her cooperating teacher settled the students for the day. While this was early in her student teaching experience, Joan suggested that Cheri read to the class the "Big Book" that was part of the day's lesson. As I watched Cheri read, I looked around and noticed the faces and actions of the children. Some were listening closely, some were poking their friends, and some wore quizzical looks on their faces as if they didn't "get it." Cheri read on, and when she concluded, her cooperating teacher continued the lesson.

Following this observation, I asked Cheri how she felt about her initial involvement in the class.

"I enjoyed reading to the children," she replied enthusiastically, "I'm really ready to teach. Do we have to observe for a whole week before we actually teach?"

I pointed out that taking over all of the classes, including planning, was a big step, and that the college recommended that the student teachers take a gradual approach to their involvement in the classroom.

"You know that I created good lessons in my methods classes," Cheri countered. "I'd really like to begin tomorrow teaching reading."

"I'll leave that up to you and your cooperating teacher to decide, Cheri," I answered, "but take your time and get comfortable with the students, learn their names, and observe how they learn before you take over too much of the teaching."

"Oh, I've been doing that yesterday and today. . . . I think I'm ready!"

After discussing this with Mrs. Robinson, she and Cheri determined that Cheri would read to the class again the next day and follow the plan that was already prepared for the reading lesson. I knew that Cheri had been unaware that some of the students had been distracted while she had been reading, so I offered a suggestion. "Why don't you get the videotape equipment set up for tomorrow, Cheri, so that Joan can tape your first lesson? Then you can tape several other lessons throughout the semester and compare and identify your development."

"Videotape myself? I hate to look at myself!" Cheri replied.

With some urging on my part, Cheri agreed, and we planned to watch the tape together in a week when I came back to see her.

The following week, I brought popcorn, and Cheri and I found a small study room off the library to view her tape. Before we started the tape, I asked her how she felt about the lesson she had taped.

"I was more nervous than I had imagined," Cheri replied. "We were doing some shared reading, I was reading out loud and had asked the children to follow along. We had a little discussion about what the story was all about, but they needed to look at the book again before they were really able to offer any answers."

Following our viewing of the tape, I asked Cheri to comment on what she had observed.

"Well, I am very excited to be teaching, but I look nervous on the tape, not excited or energetic like I thought. I'm not thrilled with my voice either. I certainly felt more professional than I sounded! It also seemed to take me a long time to get through the preliminaries of the morning, like taking attendance. I thought I was pretty efficient, but I see some of the children were being silly. If I'd been faster, maybe there wouldn't have been that much time where they were doing nothing. I also have some long pauses as I think about how I am going to ask the questions following the reading. Still, the actual reading seemed to engage most of the kids. I use voices and facial expressions that seem to show how fun the story is. I could see on the tape that some of the students were not following in their books."

"Where were the kids who were not reading along?"

Cheri backed up the tape. "Ohhh—they were sitting on the edges of the reading rug. Maybe they couldn't hear or see well enough," she commented.

"Anything else that you noticed on the tape?" I asked.

"Well, I guess I was concentrating more on the reading, and I didn't really see those kids who were off-task."

"Would you feel comfortable moving where you sit, or inviting different children to sit next to you so that you could vary your proximity to some of the children?"

"Sure, I hadn't thought of that. I do remember talking about using proximity as a management tool in my methods class, though," Cheri smiled. "Another thing—maybe if I took a bit more time between pages to look at the children, ask a question, or point out something in the illustration, I might engage them more."

Cheri had noticed that her ability to see the children's activities was somewhat limited in her first tape. I assured her that this is often the case for beginning teachers; their energies are focused on the task at hand and they do not see all of what is going on in the classroom. I reminded her that her new awareness should enable her to develop strategies for including all the children and keeping them interested in the lesson.

After a few more weeks, Cheri videotaped her teaching again. This was a math lesson, and the children were sorting items, looking for similarities to categorize them. When we watched this second tape, Cheri was quick to point out that she had jumped in and answered questions that she had asked the students before many of them had even had time to think.

"I am glad that I had more detailed questions written out, though," Cheri commented. "At first I just made up the questions as I read. Having the complete question written out eliminated that gap while I was searching for the right words to translate my question into first-grade language. That part was better, but I guess I expected immediate answers when I asked the questions. When these little people are thinking about the similarities and differences of the objects, they do need to have time to think. I feel a bit uncomfortable with the silence from them even though I was the one creating too much silence before! It's just that when I ask a question and no one seems to know, I feel as if I should tell them," Cheri sighed. "I didn't give them enough wait-time, did I?"

I smiled. Cheri's focus in this conversation had begun to shift. It was obvious that she was developing a broader vision of what was going on in the class. Remembering earlier conversations about the importance of giving the children time to think about a question indicated that her focus was shifting to an emphasis on the children's learning, and not on her teaching.

During the last week of her student teaching, Cheri again had Joan videotape her reading lesson. The change from the first tape was dramatic. Cheri had the children draw a picture for the cover of the book they were reading while she efficiently completed attendance and lunch counts. When she conducted a shared reading session, her vision went beyond the words on the page, and she quietly reminded two students that she needed them to follow along with her reading. She glanced at her notes on which she had jotted down some questions, avoiding the need for a lengthy pause to formulate her thoughts. Halfway through the book, Cheri said, "I want to sit by Joey and Tasha for a while," and she got up and moved her chair next to several children who had not been paying attention. The result was a very engaged Joey and Tasha!

"Ha! The children are really coming up with some interesting answers, aren't they?" Cheri smiled, pointing this out to me while we watched the last tape. It was clear that she was not just watching herself teach; she was observing the learning taking place in the classroom. When I asked Cheri and her cooperating teacher to comment on the videotaping process, Cheri responded, " I can really see my progress. I felt confident coming into student teaching, but the tapes showed me the areas where I could continue to improve. I didn't just have to rely on someone's comments; I could see for myself how things were going. I have to admit, I watched them several times at home. The stuff that really bugged me at first, like the sound of my voice and some of my nervous habits seemed less obvious later in the semester. I feel that I have evidence that documents my ability to teach. I also have a clearer picture of what I need to continue to work on. I still jump in with answers to questions too quickly—I saw that on the last tape. But I also see the good things that I am doing. I am even thinking about creating an edited tape from the last one we taped so that I have a sample of myself teaching for my portfolio."

Cheri's cooperating teacher, Joan, was also positive about the taping sessions. "I hesitated to point out to Cheri some of the things that I noticed during her teaching that I felt could be improved. I was worried about undermining her confidence. The tapes pointed out things that we could discuss, and Cheri herself could see exactly what I was talking about. I am not sure that all student teachers would be so willing to have themselves taped, however. It's too bad we don't have a room where the camera would be invisible. It was clear that both Cheri and the children were affected by having the camera pointed at them. The second time I brought out the camera, the children all tried to sit right in front of it. The intrusiveness of hauling in a camera is a concern, but it was very helpful in identifying areas for our conversations, and in assuring Cheri that she was indeed doing a good job."

POINTS TO PONDER

1. What areas do you consider to be strengths in your teaching? In what areas are you unsure about your abilities? Discuss how comfortable you might be viewing both the positive and negative aspects of your teaching and generate some suggestions for increasing your comfort level with this process.

2. Discuss how you could arrange for your student teaching lessons to be taped. Consider who might be available to assist you with this at your site and how you can arrange for access to equipment.

3. Consider how you can attend to the lesson you are teaching and still be aware of all that is going on in your classroom.

4. A videotape of your teaching would document your abilities. What else might you include in a portfolio to give future employers insights into your teaching?

5. Because the development of teaching skills is an ongoing process, consider how the use of videotape could assist you in your progress. What other tools or methods might you use to continue to improve your teaching? What processes are often used by school districts to gather data on teacher development?

FURTHER READING

Hopkins, W. S., & Moore, K. D. (1993). *Clinical supervision: A practical guide to student teacher supervision.* Madison, WI: Brown & Benchmark.

Levine, P., Glasser, J., & Gach, W. (1984). *The complete guide to home video production.* New York: Holt, Rinehart & Winston.

Murwin, S., & Matt, S. R. (1990). Fears prior to student teaching. *The Technology Teacher, 49,* 25–26.

Newman, J. M. (1989). *Finding our own way: Teachers exploring their assumptions.* Portsmouth, NH: Heinemann.

Schubert, W. H., & Ayers, W. C. (1992). *Teacher lore: Learning from our own experience.* New York: Longman.

Withall, J., & Wood, F. H. (1979). Taking the threat out of classroom observation and feedback. *Journal of Teacher Education, 30*(1), 55–58.

Chapter Twelve

WHAT EXACTLY IS A "C"?

SETTING

Interdisciplinary Student Teaching Seminar

FOCUS QUESTIONS

When reading this chapter, consider the following questions:

- What kind of a grading plan will you use in your classroom?

- How does your teaching methodology relate to your curriculum and your grading and assessment policy?

I can't believe that so many of the kids in my introduction to Biology class got Cs or Ds on the last test I gave them!" Rebekka exclaimed as our student teaching seminar group gathered for our weekly session. "I gave them detailed information, and the labs I set up were designed to complement the lessons, and still they didn't get it. I don't want them to fail my class! What do you do when students perform so poorly?"

Jeff commented that in his elementary setting, he didn't have to deal with that issue because students were given a "satisfactory," "unsatisfactory," or "outstanding" mark at grading time.

"But how do you determine whether they really are satisfactory or not?" Rebekka demanded.

"This sounds like an issue that we should focus on tonight," I commented. As this group's college supervisor, I had been choosing specific topics for the student teachers to discuss each week, but I was glad to let them determine what they wanted to talk about tonight. I had wanted these conversations to be based on the needs and concerns of the student teachers, but the first three weeks had been primarily directed by my agenda.

"I worked so hard," Rebekka sighed, "I made handouts and generated cooperative group projects to let them make models of cell division, and many of them still couldn't get over half of the questions right. Don't they study? Shouldn't some of the responsibility be on their shoulders to prepare for the exam?"

The group nodded their agreement and confirmed that students had to take some ownership in the learning process. "It sounds like you have been working hard to get the students involved in their learning," I said to Rebekka. "Perhaps it will help to consider your purpose in testing the students," I continued. "Maybe if we think back to our methods courses and the linkage between the objectives and the methods we use to teach, we can come up with some ideas."

"Objectives are great guides," Terri commented, "but when I give a test in my history classes, I have to get the students to tell me what they know. How do I give a grade if I don't have a way to determine how well students have mastered the material?"

"I take a look at their class work," Jeff interjected. "If my objective was for students to be able to read something and use that information to answer questions or, in other words, to comprehend what they read, I can see if they met the objective by taking a look at the work they do in class."

"That may work for elementary level students," Rebekka said, "but according to the school curriculum and the state graduation standards, these students are supposed to understand basic biological processes. Understanding cell division is one of those processes. If students cannot get above a C on this test, then they do not have a basic understanding of this process."

Jeff, our sole elementary teacher in the group, looked disgusted. "I have trouble determining what a C really is—how do you do that, Rebekka?"

"I use a variety of question types; this wasn't just a 'multiple guess' kind of assessment. The students had to identify the terminology, draw out the stages of mitosis, and describe what was happening during each stage. Each multiple-choice question was worth 3 points, each drawing was worth 5 points, and each description was also worth 5 points. Using the total points possible, I figured out a percentage that gave me the top 10% for an A, the next 10% for a B, and so on. I took a lot of time to write questions that reflected what we talked about in class. So this was not a junky test!" Rebekka insisted.

I knew that this issue was one that could intensify the perceptions of difference that existed between the elementary and secondary student teachers in our program. Our department had wrestled with the issue of secondary and elementary preservice teachers often being at odds. Elementary student teachers, who were more student centered, felt the holistic approach espoused by our elementary department was the best philosophical perspective, whereas our secondary student teachers, who were more subject centered, were concerned about students learning content effectively. I jumped in, reminding the student teachers that all educators needed to reflect on what they were doing in the classroom and consider ways to continually improve. I suggested again that perhaps it would be helpful to look at the link between the specific objective, the teaching methodology, and the assessment format.

Jeff restated his objective that focused on reading comprehension. He said that, by having the students practice this skill as he guided their search for information in what they had read and then by working first in a group and later independently, he could determine that students had meet the objective. "I have the students demonstrate that they can do the task. They answer questions based on what they have read. In that way they can demonstrate that they have met the objective, and I don't need to give a test," Jeff concluded.

"My objective is that the students know what mitosis is and that they can successfully explain and identify that process," Rebekka said.

Terri added, "I like your idea Jeff, but you said earlier that you don't have to give grades. Rebekka and I need to be able to specify whether a student has achieved an A, B, C, or whatever, to put on their grade reports."

"That's exactly what I struggle with," added Chris, who was doing his student teaching with a seventh-grade math team at a local middle school. "I set up the objectives that call for the students to do more than just 'identify' or 'recognize' some basic terms. I want the students to be able to think about the information, make connections, and use the information to solve problems that integrate what we've learned. So how do I create an assessment that identifies the grades? What is a C grade, really?"

I commented that perhaps we ought to try to define a C grade.

"A grade of C is average work," Rebekka stated.

"Well, I think that in today's system, a C is passing," Terri said.

"Having 70 to 79% of the answers correct. That was a C under the grading system that was used during most of my school years," Chris added. "But if the objective is for students to be able to solve the problems, the process they use is also part of the grade. The math team at my school gives more credit for working through the problem correctly, even if the answer is wrong. By giving points for process and answers, I think we get a better picture of what the student can do. This way, a C means that the students can't use the information very effectively."

"That may be fine in math, but in biology you have to know the terminology to be able to identify the parts and processes of living things," Rebekka said.

"Why even bother with letter grades?" Jeff asked. "Why not just provide a checklist that specifies what terms they know and don't know?"

"Because we have to have grades for the transcripts!" Rebekka shouted.

"I think that we can go around and around with this conversation," I interjected. "All of your points are valid, but we are looking at this issue from different perspectives. Rebekka, you say that your school requires letter grades. But isn't your goal to encourage all students to learn the material?"

"Of course."

"Perhaps you could give practice tests, or group tests in which the students work together to identify what they have learned."

"But then I don't know what they can do individually," Rebekka said. "They will need this information for college, and if they don't get it now, it will be much harder in subsequent biology classes."

"Maybe that's the difference in our perspectives," Jeff commented. "I want the students to see why the information we are learning is relevant in their lives today. This gives them the motivation, the interest that helps them learn. I want them to be able to use the knowledge, not just identify terms. Maybe all of your students are not college bound, or maybe they don't see the importance of the information they are learning. And another thing. I was wondering what you do if students in your class are reading at different levels. Can they all really read the text? If your students need to read to learn, how do you help them if they read poorly?"

Rebekka was silent for a moment. "I think that they should be coming to us from the lower grades prepared to read," she said. "If not, then we have remedial reading courses for those kids. When you say that some of my students just don't care if they get a good grade because they are not going to go to college, then that's all the more reason to give letter grades, so that colleges can determine which students ought to be admitted!"

"I think that we have to realize that our current educational system does ask for us to sort children for college entrance purposes," I said. "I am not sure that this system is correct, but it is in place right now. However, if our goal is to help all students learn, I wonder if sorting them into A, B, C, D, and F categories provides motivation that encourages all students to engage in the learning."

"Those who get low grades will know that they need to study harder," Rebekka said.

Jeff interjected, "Do you think that remedial, low-level courses will inspire these kids with low grades to work harder?"

"Well, I think that when they have more appropriate curriculum they can get a grade that reflects their ability in that class, and they feel successful," Rebekka answered.

"But you said earlier that grades were needed for college. Will an A in remedial reading help a student get into college?" Jeff asked.

"Probably not. The course that is taken is also important."

"Okay, okay," I interrupted. I knew that this issue is difficult for many student teachers to handle. Much of their vision of teaching is based on their own prior experiences. Secondary and elementary preparation programs often are not able to counteract the preconceived notion that secondary teaching focuses on content whereas elementary teaching can be more student centered. I continued, "What if the students just don't do well in testing situations? What if they don't see the relevance of history or biology in their lives? What if their concerns center around if Mom will keep her job or if they can get home from school without getting shot? What if they get Ds on their report card—does this mean they aren't learning?"

Chris said, "In our middle school, we give practice tests so students are clear about what they will have to do on a math test. We let them read with a partner if they have trouble reading, too. But much of their final grade is determined by their ability to use the math in a real project. They work with other kids, and this project, as well as the tests, determines their grades."

"A practice test doesn't make the kids responsible for their own learning," Rebekka said.

"But if they can be more successful, isn't that good? Perhaps the competition for grades isn't healthy for our students," Chris concluded.

I mentioned that using cooperative learning was a group teaching technique, and that perhaps the evaluation ought to match more closely the teaching methodology. "If your goal is to have students be responsible for their own learning, then why have them in groups? Perhaps offering a variety of assessments and giving points for projects and group work as well as tests would help to deemphasize the test itself. The grade could then be more reflective of what the student knows and is able to do."

Rebekka shook her head. I realized that this discussion was asking her and the other students to shift their thinking to some degree. I wondered how much impact our conversation would have on Rebekka. Did debates like this open doors for student teachers and encourage them to look at their teaching from a different perspective? Or had we just fallen back into our pro-subject versus pro-student perspectives? As we concluded our meeting, I encouraged all four of the student teachers to think about this issue in the context of their own classroom and to reflect on their thoughts in their journal. I added that I would talk to each of them individually at my next observation about this topic of evaluating students.

After the students left, I silently hoped I would see some changes in the testing in Rebekka's and Terri's classrooms. Such changes would be difficult. Rebekka's cooperating teacher often encouraged students to "learn the material because it was on the test," and she was fairly traditional in her grading. I knew I believed in using a broader perspective to evaluate students and that we had emphasized alternative assessment in our methods classes. How would the realities of the classroom and conversations with colleagues who presented differing perspectives shape the assessment practices of students like Rebekka? I sighed and wondered if the "change process" for these students could be accelerated. Despite the difficulty of facilitating discussions such as the one we'd had this evening, I really believe that if Rebekka and students like her are not challenged to carefully consider their educational decisions, our schools will not be able to improve education for all children.

 ## POINTS TO PONDER

1. What is your philosophy regarding grading? Define the kind of evaluative practices you will you use to determine if your students are learning. Be specific.

2. How important are grades? Should the emphasis on grades be different for elementary and secondary students?

3. Discuss the linkage between curriculum's objectives, the methodology used to teach, and the evaluation process. How do these connections affect how you assess students?

4. Consider how you will interact with colleagues, both student teachers and other certified teachers, who espouse educational philosophies that differ from your own. What kind of impact can you have on the teaching practices of others?

5. Do you consider yourself to be a student-centered teacher or a content-focused teacher? Why? What does it mean to use "developmentally appropriate" teaching methods?

6. What risks are involved in trying to generate positive change in a system that might not be open to your ideas? How can you minimize these risks?

7. How can you ensure that you remain aware and open to new educational practices that can have a positive impact on the learning of children?

8. What should secondary teachers do to continue to support the development of reading skills for their students? How will you approach teaching reading in the content area you teach? How can elementary and secondary teachers work together to ensure a seamless curriculum for students in kindergarten through high school?

 ## FURTHER READING

Alverman, D. (1981). The possible value of dissonance in student teaching experiences. *Journal of Teacher Education, 32*(3), 24–25.

Barnes, S. (1985). A study of classroom pupil evaluation: The missing link in teacher education. *Journal of Teacher Education, 36*(4), 46–49.

Bullough, R., Knowles, J., & Crow, N. (1989). Teacher self-concept and student culture in the first year of teaching. *Teachers College Press, 91*(2), 209–233.

Redirecting assessment. (1989). *Educational Leadership, 46*(7), 2–77.

Slavin, R. (1991). *Student team learning: A practical guide to cooperative learning.* Washington, DC: National Education Association.

Vavrus, L. (1990). Put portfolios to the test. *Instructor, 100*(1), 48–53.

Chapter Thirteen

I GET NO RESPECT

SETTING

Second-Grade Classroom, Urban School

FOCUS QUESTIONS

While reading this case, consider the following questions:

- What is your view of control in the classroom?
- How do you plan to interact with the children in your classroom to develop a relationship that fosters respect?

The phone rang and I reached for it, wondering who would be calling this late at night. I gave out my home phone number to all of my student teachers, knowing that they often needed to connect with me outside of the school day. After I said, "Hello," I heard Kayla Carter, one of my student teachers, announce that she needed some help.

"What's up?" I asked, and Kayla responded that she didn't feel that she was getting any respect from her students or the other teachers in her building. I asked her to give me some examples of what she meant, and she hesitated.

"Well, for one thing, Derek Halpner, my cooperating teacher, has a loud, intense way of talking to these kids. I have a strong voice, too, but my style is more subdued. He frequently 'talks over me' and gives the children additional directions. If I have kids who come in with a note from their folks, or if they need to go to the bathroom, they continue to go to Mr. Halpner's desk in the back of the room and ask him for permission. He has directed them back to me, but sometimes he handles the problem, and I am not sure where I stand. I just wonder if maybe because most of the students are African American, and so is Derek, that I am not really being taken seriously. I am supposed to be the teacher here, and I don't think that the kids respect me when they continually are allowed to go to Mr. Halpner to get things done."

I asked Kayla if she felt comfortable with the relationship she and her cooperating teacher had established during the first four weeks of this experience. She said that she did, but it annoyed her that he kept stepping in and "helping out."

"You know, children that age really feel attached to their teacher," I responded. "I don't think that Derek is trying to undermine your teaching, but I do think that you need to talk to him about how you feel."

"But that's just it," Kayla replied. "Whenever I try to get serious about an issue, he just smiles and says that when I have my own class, I'll understand things better. How am I ever going to have my own class if I don't get a chance to handle things now?"

After asking a few more questions, I determined that Kayla felt Derek was patronizing her and her ideas. She had wanted to introduce some alternative groupings of the children for reading and use some trade books to bring a more whole language approach to this subject. Derek had smiled and told her that all of the fads in education had come and gone, and that he was committed to teaching these kids how to read so they could do something with their lives. Kayla and Derek had both articulated their concern and commitment to children who came from difficult backgrounds. One of the reasons Kayla had wanted to teach with Derek was that she felt, as he did, that a safe, supportive classroom was the key to enabling children to learn, and that education was the way that these kids could have a better life. Kayla had often expressed interest in creating positive learning environments in diverse settings. She had written and spoken about infusing her curriculum with multicultural materials. I believed that Kayla could handle this classroom setting, so I told her I would stop at her school the next day to talk about her concerns more in depth.

The next day, over lunch with both of them, I asked Derek if he had any issues regarding Kayla's teaching that he would like to discuss. He assured me that she was very good with the children, but that he didn't want her to alter his curriculum.

"These kids need a systematic approach to help them read. All of this whole language stuff keeps kids from getting into the hard work of learning to read. I realize that not everyone shares this belief, but I don't think that using the kid's own language gives them the decoding skills they need to face more difficult vocabulary—and then they can't progress. I am determined that the kids who leave my classroom are going to be equipped with the skills to be successful readers. Feeling sorry for these kids and making things easy is not the way to help them be successful in school. I know. I've lived this experience."

"So you would rather that Kayla continue with the approach that you use in the classroom?" I asked.

"She can try a lesson or two if she would like, but she needs to understand that these kids may not come from background where their parents read to them, so they need a different, more skill-based approach to learning. I just think she hasn't had enough experience to know what to teach in a school like this. She'll get wiser with more time in the trenches."

Kayla rolled her eyes at me when she heard this, and I knew that she was not happy with how the conversation was going. I asked Derek if perhaps it might be helpful for Kayla to begin to handle all of the students' questions and requests in the classroom, so that she could experience the full scope of the teachers' responsibilities.

"Sure," he replied, "but she may be overwhelmed. I know she has been working at another job to pay tuition fees on the weekends, and that she has already caught one cold from the kids so far. The reality of the classroom is that you have to be fully committed to teaching; you have to constantly be thinking about how you are going to teach the next day's lesson. The intensity of this and the neediness of the kids can be draining. I don't think that she is up to that yet, and so I am trying to run interference for her by picking up the slack."

Kayla spoke up at that point and asked that she be given the chance to try to handle things. She was as intense as Derek was, and I wondered if they might not work better together, rather than at opposite poles.

"What if you work as a team and rotate the duties and teaching tasks each day or by the week," I suggested. "Then Derek can provide support and you can demonstrate the whole language approach that integrates the use of decoding skills."

Derek was supportive of this idea, but Kayla still wanted control of the classroom. We talked a while more and then decided that a team approach might be a good way to start. Then when Derek felt it appropriate, he would leave Kayla in the classroom to handle things herself.

The team-teaching went well, although Kayla still reported that she felt that she didn't get enough respect from the children or from Derek. "What do you mean?" I asked during one of our conferences.

"Well, he is always giving me his all-knowing smile when something goes wrong—sort of an 'I told you so' without words. He insists on more time for the skills aspect of reading, and I want to read books with the children and have them read with me, so that they enjoy reading and don't get so bored with all the nonsense sentences on those skill sheets."

"Why did you ask to work with Derek if you have such a different philosophy of teaching?" I asked Kayla finally.

"I knew from friends that kids learned in Derek's classroom. I appreciate someone who is committed to teaching. You said that we should use what we know is "best practice" in our teaching during this experience, and that is what I am trying to do. Derek says that the kids need the skills because they have less preparation coming into school; I say that is precisely the reason I need to read to them more than he allows me time to do! They need a print-rich environment at school if they don't have one at home."

I was worried that these two were headed for a major confrontation, but then Kayla took over the classroom by herself. Kayla was still working on weekends, and it was obvious that she was getting physically run down. When I reminded her that it was important to stay healthy so that she would be effective in the classroom, she told me that she was capable of handling things. Then came the day when the teachers learned that one of the students in the school, a sixth grader, had killed himself.

Kayla called me later that night and told me that she was informed before school that the kids might need some support, and that the school counselor was going to try to get to all of the classrooms. Obviously though, the counselor wanted to spend most of her time with the sixth graders. When the children arrived at school, they were already talking about the situation, and Kayla was unsure of what to do.

"When I saw the tears on the faces of these kids and heard them recount stories of other deaths they had already experienced in their short lives, I was so depressed. Maybe it was the lack of sleep, but I just felt so overwhelmed that I cried! Derek came in and together we asked the children what they wanted to do that day. They wanted to make cards for the boy's family, so we helped them write messages and let them draw their own designs. I know this wasn't what was planned, but we just couldn't force the kids to work that day. We offered the kids what support we could, and we talked about all the reasons for living, trying to counter the message of suicide," she said.

I assured Kayla that she had done the right thing, that children needed to discuss tragedies, not ignore them.

Following that experience, Kayla said that the kids seemed to be more satisfied with her directing the classroom. Fewer of the children asked where Derek was when he was out of the room, and she felt more in charge.

"The problem is that, while the kids may give me more respect, I feel as if I have lost Derek's respect totally. I mean, I cried!! How responsible is that for a teacher, when I can't even control my own emotions?"

At that point, it hit me that maybe the respect issue was really one of control. Kayla seemed to think that if she controlled everything in the classroom, if she had the power to determine everything, she would be respected by the children and by her cooperating teacher. We talked for a few minutes, and I suggested that perhaps by losing control, so to speak, by crying, she actually won the respect of the children, and Derek.

"What do you mean?" she asked.

"Well, often we have a vision of teaching that says that the teacher has to be in control and have the final say—in what the children are allowed to do, in curriculum, in everything. And while teachers need to make decisions, those decisions can be better if we allow those involved to have some say in what is going to happen. I am sure that the children appreciated your letting them choose how to respond the day after the suicide."

"But kids can't determine what is best for themselves. Teachers have to do that!" Kayla replied.

"True, but you can let them have some say in what is going on. The same goes for working with other faculty. When you and Derek worked together on the reading lessons, did you think he was as strongly opposed to the idea of whole language as before?"

When Kayla agreed that Derek had been open to meeting her half way on the language curriculum, I pointed out that this was an example of sharing the decision-making process. When she had stopped her overt comments about the need for whole language over a phonetic approach and was willing to share the control over content decisions, the children benefited. "Collaborative teaching and opportunities to engage in dialogue with colleagues helps teachers see a variety of perspectives," I said. "All those involved in what goes on in the classroom have to work together before learning takes place. You earn respect by giving respect. Giving respect to the children for what they bring to the classroom and giving respect to other teachers for their years of wisdom and point of view is important," I said.

Kayla paused for a moment and then told me she'd have to think about my comments.

When I observed Kayla during her last week of teaching, she was infusing decoding strategies into her "big book" lessons and stated that this integrated approach seemed to best meet the needs of all of the kids. She told me that she and Derek were getting along better as well.

"I see now that he was trying to help me by handling some of the 'housekeeping' tasks in the classroom, so that I could concentrate on what I was doing—teaching! I guess I was kind of hung up on the idea that the classroom in which I did my student teaching would be MY classroom. I wanted the experience of controlling a classroom so badly that I think I overreacted to Derek's comments. While it seemed patronizing at first, I realize Derek is a caring, concerned person. Maybe I was a little put off by our different cultural perspectives. I probably came across as wanting to be the savior for these kids, and maybe I acted a little bit superior in my attitude. I still think that Derek is working from an outdated model, but I know he is deeply committed to the children in his classroom, and he wanted me to demonstrate that same depth of commitment. I was still focused on controlling the classroom, and I wanted him to step totally out of the picture. Derek's support, especially on the day of the suicide, was vital in my own development."

"You had been worried about crying in front of Derek that day," I reminded her, "how did you deal with that issue?"

Kayla smiled, "Derek told me that he knew I was a good teacher after that day. He told me he respected me more, because it was the first time I showed any real empathy in the classroom. My concern with control kept me from becoming emotionally attached to the children, and maybe that's the way I wanted it, at first. The day I shared their grief, Derek said he saw that I had the heart of a teacher, after all. He told me that experience showed him that I didn't place myself above the kids but that I was connected with them. We have spent more time talking about our philosophies, and we're both willing to see the other's perspective on the whole language issue. Now I feel more like a colleague than his student teacher."

"What conclusions did you come to about your different methodologies?" I asked.

Kayla responded,"True whole language includes some decoding, but I wasn't focusing on that component because of the need to incorporate literature. Blending our viewpoints enabled Derek and me to come up with an approach that seems to work." She paused a moment. "I think that when I have my own classroom, though, I will focus more on whole language. I won't ignore decoding skills, but I truly believe that the use of literature in the whole language approach is a better method for teaching reading than the old phonics system."

Kayla thanked me for my help and strode confidently back to her classroom. As I watched her go, I shook my head. I wondered if she was fully aware of the need to be flexible in her teaching to respond to children's varying levels of development. I did not believe that one method of teaching would meet the needs of all children. I also wondered how our educational program at the college could work to develop a higher level of comfort for white students as they worked in multicultural settings. Kayla still had room to grow as a teacher, and I hoped she would remain open to other ideas and perspectives. She would also have to decide about the issue of control in her classroom.

I know the goal of the college is to develop self-confident teachers, but I wondered what Kayla would do when she got her first job. What if she was hired by a district that used basal readers? How would she fit into an urban setting? Could she interact effectively with teachers and parents of color? How would she respond to directives from a principal? Would she be a teacher who could continue to learn and grow, or was she so set in her methods of teaching that she could not see the benefits of new ideas and differing philosophies? I wondered if, five or ten years from now, Kayla would be a "good" teacher?

POINTS TO PONDER

1. What do you think lies ahead in Kayla's teaching career? Does she need to be flexible or should she continue to insist on the superiority of her teaching methodology?

2. What is the role of power and control in the classroom?

3. What is your understanding of the cultural differences that are present in your school setting? How will this affect your teaching? Consider the culture of the two teachers involved in this case. What affect might cross-cultural communication have had in this situation? Consider your own reaction in such a situation. Consider how the situation might differ if the cultural backgrounds of the two teachers had been reversed.

4. What is your position in the debate between whole language and phonics instruction? How will you defend your position on this issue to teachers and administrators who have differing opinions?

5. What role do you expect your cooperating teacher to play in your student teaching experience? How important is mutual respect in this relationship? How should teaching colleagues treat each other when they disagree?

6. How would you deal with tragedies in the classroom? What should the teacher's role be? What supports are available for children when a crisis arises like the one described in this case?

7. How will you earn the respect of the children in your classroom?

FURTHER READING

Berscheid, E. (1983). Emotion. In H. Kelley, E. Berscheid, & A. Christensen et. al. (Eds.), *Close Relationships*, (pp. 110–168). New York: W. H. Freeman.

Burke, R. (1970). Methods of resolving superior-subordinate conflict: The constructive use of subordinate differences and disagreements. *Organizational Behavior and Human Performance, 5*, 393–411.

Carlson, J., & Thorpe, C. (1984). Communication: Learning to give and take. *The growing teacher: How to become the teacher you've always wanted to be.* Englewood Cliffs, NJ: Prentice-Hall.

Maeroff, G. (1993). *Team building for school change.* New York: Teachers College Press.

Samorar, L., Porter, R., & Nemi, J. (1981). *Understanding intercultural communication.* Belmont, CA: Wadsworth.

Weaver, C. (1990). *Understanding whole language: From principles to practice.* Portsmouth, NH: Heinemann.

Chapter Fourteen

WE DON'T DO GROUP WORK HERE

SETTING

High School Mathematics Department

FOCUS QUESTIONS

When reading this case, consider the following questions:

- What teaching methods do you intend to use when you are student teaching?

- How can a student teacher be an agent of change in a school?

Terri came to our last class session of the semester, beaming. She told us that she had gotten her first choice for her student teaching placement. She had been involved in that particular school for many years, having served there as a volunteer math tutor since her first year in college. The woman who was to be her cooperating teacher, Nancy Stutz, was someone Terri had worked with extensively in the tutoring sessions. Terri was going to be Nancy's first student teacher, and they both were pleased with the comfort level that existed in their relationship. In January Terri would begin teaching freshman Algebra, and she had some very definite ideas about how her students would learn.

Terri had been strongly influenced by a previous course, educational psychology, where the instructor had presented the concept of cooperative learning. The students had been given group quizzes, and Terri had enthusiastically applied this concept to her field of mathematics in this methods class. Her practice lessons were very dynamic, and she managed the group process very effectively. Terri told me that she was planning to use cooperative learning in her student teaching assignment because it supported her belief that the process of mathematics was far more valuable to students than getting the right answer.

One night, halfway through the next semester, Terri appeared at my office door. "How's it going?" I asked, referring to her student teaching.

"Well, I'm having to work through the rules and regulations that seem to be in place before I can implement any cooperative learning," she said, "and that's a bit frustrating."

Knowing that Terri had hand-picked her student teaching placement, I asked, "What do you mean?"

"Well, Nancy is a good teacher, and her structure was very important when we were working with students in the tutoring sessions, but she is really reluctant to make any changes with the whole class." Terri responded. "She said that she is concerned that I don't know enough about cooperative learning since I was just exposed to it in one college class. But I have read a lot about this stuff, and I came up with some cooperative lessons for our methods class, remember?"

"I sure do, Terri," I said. "You generated some very exciting lessons that clearly taught the concept, but went beyond that and enabled students to hear other ideas about how to solve a problem."

Terri sighed, saying, "That's one of my objectives, to let students know that there are sometimes several ways to come up with an answer. I also want them to have to talk about the process, so that they understand why they got their answer. Nancy told me that the principal doesn't like cooperative learning, and she asked me to call my little experiences 'group work' because I couldn't possibly be experienced enough to implement real cooperative learning."

"Do you think that Nancy understands what cooperative learning is all about?" I asked Terri.

"Well, I think she is concerned about the students learning on their own. I want to give a group quiz, or practice, before the graded quiz. The groups would work together to solve problems just like the ones that would be on the graded quiz. The students would need to be able to explain how they got the answers, and we might even work a few together on the board afterwards to clear up any confusing areas. I know that this idea meets two of the criteria for cooperative learning: individual accountability and group interdependence. I have a quick way of getting the rows to turn and form small sets of four, so I have also thought about the cooperative learning requirement for face-to-face interaction. With so much emphasis on the grade, I suppose that this group work might seem like cheating. I look at it another way: to ensure that everybody knows the material."

"So how are you dealing with this?" I asked.

"Well, I know Nancy well enough that I have been comfortable with talking up the idea of cooperative learning—and I think I'm wearing her down a bit. And now that she is not in the room all of the time, I have been giving group quizzes anyway."

"Aren't you concerned that Nancy might find this a bit subversive? After all, it is her classroom," I said.

"But this is also my student teaching experience!" Terri cried. "I need to work the bugs out of my teaching now so that I will be ready when I get my own class-room. If I can't try cooperative learning lessons and consider what works and what doesn't, how will I be ready to use this method when I get a job?"

"What about the evaluation that you will be getting from Nancy at the end of the semester?" I asked. Thinking of difficult situations I had heard of that resulted from friction between the student teacher and the cooperating teacher, I contin-ued, "Aren't you concerned that she may give you an evaluation that would inter-fere with your ability to get a teaching job? What if she says that you are 'some-one who can't work well with other teachers', or who is 'unresponsive to the wishes of the administration'?"

"I really don't think that Nancy would do that to me," Terri responded. "We've worked together for long time, and she knows that we have different philosophies of teaching. She really values quiet and order, and I'm always get-ting the students riled up and having them debate the way we work through a problem. I think that they have to be involved in the learning. Nancy would rather that her students sit quietly and watch her solve the problems on the over-head and then do exactly the same thing on their homework and their tests that she did in her explanation. If a kid doesn't understand Nancy's explanation, it's too bad for them. She expects kids to do most of their learning on their own; I expect them to ask each other and figure things out together."

"If you have such different styles of teaching, why did you ask to student teach with Nancy?" I inquired.

"I knew that I would be comfortable with Nancy and this school because I had been there working with her a lot. There is too much else that is new in stu-dent teaching; I wanted to have some things that were familiar. Nancy's teaching differences are familiar—it wasn't really a shock to me that she was not enthusi-astic about cooperative learning," Terri said.

"So you are willing to take such a risk?" I asked again.

"I don't look at it as a risk," Terri countered. "I want to try cooperative learn-ing in my Algebra classes, and Nancy will let me, even if she isn't too keen on it. I suppose if she absolutely forbids me to try it, I will have some concerns, but I know Nancy won't oppose my efforts."

"Let me know how it goes," I called to Terri as she left. I still wasn't convinced that Terri was making the right choice. We often talked in class about being agents of change, of holding to your beliefs about children and the way they learn, even if teachers and administrators are not supportive of the new perspective. But I didn't want Terri to jeopardize her future, and getting a poor evaluation from your cooperating teacher could have severe ramifications. Were we setting our students up for failure if we encouraged them to struggle against the wishes of their cooperating teacher? Should student teachers be agents of change—or should they wait until they have job security? I wondered if they waited and didn't try to implement new methodology early on, if they would become complacent and fall into the patterns of the other teachers around them. I jotted myself a note to speak with the professor who was supervising Terri to see what he thought about this issue. In any case, I was proud of Terri for having the strength of her convictions. I knew that she would be a wonderful teacher and a great asset to a school district—if she survived student teaching!

When I called Ward Douglas, one of my colleagues who was supervising student teachers this semester, he assured me that Terri was in no danger of receiving a poor teaching evaluation. He said that the cooperating teacher was somewhat tenuous in her comments, but that the friendship the two had established enabled Nancy to support Terri's use of cooperative learning. Relieved, I dropped a note of support in the mail for Terri and asked her to fill me in on her experience at the end of the term.

On a sunny day in May, a few days before graduation, Terri stopped into my office. "I've got a job!" she announced.

"Where?"

"At Eisenhower, the school where I student taught," she answered, enthusiastically.

"That's wonderful, Terri!" I replied. "I was a bit concerned about your situation after we talked earlier, but it sounds as if you had a very successful experience!"

"I really did," Terri continued, sitting down to give me the details. "When I took over all the Algebra classes, I used a group 'quiz' review system, and I often put the students into groups to work on problem sets. Nancy told me she wouldn't use cooperative learning, but if I felt that strongly about it, she would let me try it during the four weeks that I handled the class alone. The results on the chapter tests showed that the class didn't fall apart; in fact, a few kids actually did better than they had previously. I might even have Nancy convinced. She let me rearrange the classroom to put the students permanently in groups of three."

"Was there any question about the grading of students who worked cooperatively?" I asked.

"I used a combination of group grades and individual assessment, just like my college text specified. Each week the groups had a problem to solve that relied on information given during earlier lessons. I observed them working on this project and gave them time to discuss how everyone was working. If someone was not involved or didn't do his or her share of the work, I'd have a little chat with that person after class. It helped that I arranged the groups at the beginning, so that I had some idea that the students involved would be able to function reasonably well together. In addition, if the whole group got a grade that was a 9 or 10, they could all get an extra point on their individual grade. This really got them working!"

"I also devised roles for everyone, again, based on the idea of group interdependence. We rotated these jobs, so that for each project, the kids had different tasks."

"Your organization and persistence paid off!" I said. "Now tell me, how did the job offer come about?"

Terri smiled. "Nancy asked the principal to come and observe the 'group work' that I did. The day I was observed by the principal, I was really nervous, but at least I didn't know at the time that there was an opening in the Math department. I would have been tempted to revert to a lecture instead of using the cooperative lesson I had planned if I'd know what was at stake! Later, the principal asked me to interview for the opening they would have in freshman Algebra! He said that he was interested in seeing the long-term effects of this method of teaching, so maybe it was the group learning that got me the job. Next year Nancy and I will be colleagues. She knows I'm going to bug her about cooperative learning—who knows, maybe I'll convert the whole department!"

◉ POINTS TO PONDER

1. If your cooperating teacher does not hold the same teaching philosophy you do, how will this affect your teaching?

2. If you had the opportunity to select your own cooperating teacher, what factors would you consider in making that decision?

3. How can you establish a comfortable relationship with your cooperating teacher before you begin your student teaching experience?

4. What teaching methods do you want to implement in your teaching during your student teaching semester? How will you handle a situation like Terri's where your cooperating teacher is not supportive of your teaching methods?

5. Can a single teacher generate interest in a new teaching method and foster change within the school?

6. Is it a realistic expectation to ask student teachers to be agents of change? As a student teacher, what risks and challenges must you face in your role as an agent of change?

FURTHER READING

Lyman, L., & Foyle, H. (1990). *Cooperative grouping for interactive learning: Students, teachers and administrators.* Washington, DC: National Education Association.

Patterson, J. (1993). *Leadership for tomorrow's schools.* Alexandria, VA: Association for Supervision and Curriculum Development.

Maeroff, G. (1993). *Team building for school change.* New York: Teachers College Press.

Schwebel, A. et. al. (1992). Relationship with the cooperating teacher: The foundation of effective student teaching. *The student teacher's handbook.* Hillsdale, NJ: Lawrence Erlbaum Associates.

Slavin, R. (1991). *Student team learning: A practical guide to cooperative learning.* Washington, DC: National Education Association.

Chapter Fifteen

FIRST IMPRESSIONS

SETTING

Third Grade

FOCUS QUESTIONS

When reading this case, consider the following questions:

- What can you do to prepare yourself for the student teaching experience?
- How can you help generate the kind of relationship and interaction with your cooperating teacher that you would like to have?

As I completed James's evaluation form for his placement file, I thought back over the past semester. James had been in Sally March's third-grade class in a suburban school district close to the college, and I had really enjoyed visiting their classroom. I looked over what I had written about his teaching and smiled, remembering the time he had gotten the students so excited about math by having them find geometric shapes in pictures. The children kept saying that this was like an art lesson, and James had pointed out that math was related to many of the things around them. The class had then gone on to draw pictures that incorporated geometric shapes to reinforce their understanding of the various spatial forms.

James had many lessons like that one which indicated his potential. He was a good beginning teacher, conscientious and hard working. When a suggestion was made to him, he worked on that aspect of his teaching and asked for more feedback. The reason I enjoyed observing him was that there never seemed to be any major crises that erupted. Student teachers often are unable to deal with differing opinions in the classroom, and I was often placed in the role of mediator between the cooperating teacher and the student teacher. This made my job as college supervisor more difficult. I viewed my role as an advocate for the student teacher, but I recognized that the classroom teacher was responsible for what went on in the classroom. Some licensed teachers were very rigid in their viewpoints, and some student teachers were unable to pull together their lessons. This mixture of perspectives, abilities, and experience often created an arena in which the two players bobbed and weaved around their differences. While the cooperating teacher and the student teacher worked well together in many circumstances, more often than not I had to smooth out rough waters so that both parties could focus on the student teacher's development. These situations were emotionally draining, and that is why I had enjoyed the respite in James's classroom. Observing James, I never had to worry about difficulties that might lie below the surface. That was due to James's conscious effort to approach his student teaching experience in a proactive way. Rather than wait to see what developed, he had carefully planned to establish a comfortable communication process for all parties involved in his student teaching experience.

One incident in particular highlighted the effectiveness of James's approach. After the lesson using art and geometric figures, a parent called to report that his daughter had come home and announced that they weren't having math anymore. James defused an initially angry phone call when he explained the lesson and the connection between art and mathematical shapes. The father ended the conversation feeling reassured that his daughter was, indeed, still being taught math. This incident had all the ingredients for the making of a major difficulty. James, however, had opened the door to allow for effective communication by sending a letter home to parents prior to starting his student teaching. I believe that letter helped keep this misunderstanding from becoming a larger incident.

January 15, 1993

Dear Parent(s)/Guardian(s):

This letter is to introduce myself to you. My name is James Koster and I am a student teacher for Mrs. March's third grade class. I will be graduating from Northern College in May with a B.A. in Elementary Education. Although my specialty area is science, I feel that I am very qualified to teach all subjects to your son or daughter.

The second semester will be spent continuing the curriculum that Mrs. March has begun. We will be adding a writing workshop to our language arts curriculum, and I want the students to begin to read books of their own choosing. I will use a journal to encourage the students to write about what they read; we will complete an independent project over the book that each student selects. I will be using a lot of hands-on math and science projects, and we will use our social studies time to focus on geography. I hope that you can stimulate your child's learning by sharing with him or her some of your own experiences that relate to the topics we will be studying. Please feel free to sit in on any class, or to contact me with any suggestions for our classes. I am always willing to listen to new ideas.

Finally, please feel free to call me here at school or at home about any questions or concerns. My home number is 720-8139. (Please call before 10:00 p.m.) I am also available in room 208 from 7:45–8:00 a.m. I will have limited time after school hours because I will be helping coach the high school baseball team. However, if there is a definite need for me to stay after school to assist students, then I will make time for them. I hope that these final few months of school will be very valuable for your child as well as for me. Thank you for your time!

Sincerely,

James Coster

I took the letter from James' file and reread it. The letter created a first impression that enabled both the parents and the cooperating teacher to feel comfortable in approaching James about concerns and issues. Sally told me during one of our conversations that James's willingness to honestly convey his plans and his schedule made it clear that he was organized and effective, and it made her feel that he was indeed open to hearing ideas other than his own.

James had shown her a draft of the letter on his first pre-student teaching visit after he had been assigned to her classroom.

"That letter served as a beginning for us. Knowing that James was busy after school might have been a concern for me in his position as my student teacher," the cooperating teacher had said. "I don't like student teachers who rush off after classes are dismissed. But James had clearly identified the time conflict and offered alternative times and methods for communicating. This worked well for me, as I often had meetings before and after school. While we had a brief conference every day at lunch, I knew that I could call James when things came up that we needed to discuss. I also liked the fact that parents were aware that there was a student teacher in the room, and that he would be following our curriculum while at the same time bringing in some new ideas. At one point during the semester, I was somewhat concerned about the loose structure in the writing lab, so I called James that evening to discuss options for tightening things up, and we worked out a plan that made me feel more comfortable without negatively impacting his approach."

"On several occasions parents called James directly," Sally continued. "This gave him a real sense of ownership in the class as well as experience in dealing with parents. I made sure that he filled me in so I could assist with issues beyond his expertise, but his letter served as a professional introduction to parents, and it reflected positively on his work throughout the semester."

As I looked over my notes from James's teaching experience, I recalled the way he had created a positive first impression with Sally by meeting her several times prior to the beginning of his experience and discussing their philosophies of teaching as well as his goals for student teaching. I sat in on one of these initial meetings to go over the expectations from the college for the student teaching experience. James and Sally talked about how James would be acclimated into the classroom and teaching, which classes he would take over first, and when they would meet each day to review lesson plans. Sally had initially been somewhat vague about when she and James would get together, but James had specifically asked for daily contact, saying "I want us to be a team, and I will feel more comfortable if we check in each day to be sure that we are comfortable with the upcoming lessons."

James had lots of innovations that he wanted to try, and he talked to Sally about how she felt about each idea. He brought a checklist with him to that first meeting to be sure they talked about all of his ideas and concerns. Sally asked him to initially focus on direct instruction and then move to the cooperative lessons and projects that he described. James also had templates from his methods classes of various kinds of lesson plans that he wanted to try out, but Sally wanted to use a Madeline Hunter model. James then asked if he could try other lesson plan formats later on, so he could develop a flexible approach to planning. This seemed to be a new idea to Sally, but after emphasizing that James needed to master the Hunter model, she agreed that he could try alternate ideas after they had discussed them and agreed upon them for each day. Clarifying these issues up front enabled James to use a format that was comfortable for his cooperating teacher, while allowing the novice teacher to develop his own style in the classroom.

This initial conversation was definitely a two-way dialogue, with James clarifying what he wanted to do during his experience and Sally expressing her concerns and expectations. After sitting in on this meeting, I felt very confident that James had opened a clear path for communicating with Sally that would enable them to work through differences in their daily meetings. What was interesting to me was that the college specifically asked all student teachers to set up meetings to begin to develop a relationship with their cooperating teacher prior to beginning their work in the schools. Why was it that James found this so easy to do, while many student teachers refused to take the time and then ended up frustrated when communication with the cooperating teacher broke down?

During this pre-student teaching meeting, James also asked if he could meet the principal, and Sally took him down to the main office for an introduction that resulted in an informal tour of the building as well as an offer from the principal to drop in and give James feedback on his teaching. This kind of support from the administration was encouraging. And while I always ask student teachers to try to meet their administrators, James was assertive in making these connections *before* he began his teaching.

As I reflected on James's student teaching experience, it occurred to me that James had progressed so well in his skill development because he had established a positive relationship with his cooperating teacher. Through their daily chats, Sally and James had achieved an understanding of each other's perspectives that enabled them to discuss differences comfortably. The parents and principal were comfortable with James because he had initiated contact with them and he wasn't a complete unknown in the classroom. Paying attention to relationship building is something we recommend in cooperative learning. Why did we place so little emphasis on this in student teaching, which is, in essence, a very cooperative effort? The working relationship between the cooperating teacher and the student teacher is vitally important. Could tensions be eliminated by getting to know one another before the student teacher began the difficult work of teaching?

Perhaps, as the college supervisor, my role should be to assist in relationship building prior to student teaching. It would certainly be worth my time to work out a way to encourage all student teachers to put together a specific communication plan and thus avoid the fallout that can occur when the student teacher and cooperating teacher are unable to deal with their differences. I wondered about the kinds of interpersonal skills that could be fostered during education coursework to give students the ability and confidence to initiate meetings like those James had with Sally. Perhaps the college needs to spend more time on interactive communication processes and team-building skills so that our future teachers can be assertive and create a positive first impression. While this approach may not work for everyone, it may help build a positive relationship between all parties involved in the student teaching experience. Now . . . I only have to figure out what to take out of our education coursework to provide time for interpersonal communication!

POINTS TO PONDER

1. How comfortable would you be with taking a proactive role in developing a positive relationship with your future cooperating teacher? What skills do you think you need to enable you to feel confident with such an approach?

2. Reread James's letter. Would you add or change anything if you were sending out a letter of greeting to the parents of the children in your future classes?

3. How will you work out differences between you and your cooperating teacher? How do you see the role of the college supervisor in these situations?

4. What format(s) will you use for developing your lesson plans during student teaching?

5. Where do you think the development of interpersonal communication skills should fit into your education coursework? Can work on these skills be tied to studies of cooperative learning?

6. What role will you take in shaping your student teaching experience? How will you communicate this role to your cooperating teacher?

   • Will you be experimental and try new methodologies and ideas?
   • Will you teach what you know you can do in a way in which you are comfortable?
   • Will you follow the lead of your cooperating teacher and model yourself after him or her?
   • Will you do what is asked of you by the college and the cooperating teacher? Will you do more?
   • Will you develop goals for yourself during student teaching?
   • Will you be comfortable with other individuals, such as principals, team leaders, and other teachers observing you and giving you feedback?
   • Will you develop relationships with other educators in your building and draw on their expertise as you teach?
   • Will you focus on teaching and classroom interactions, or will you try to take on the total teaching role by assisting with extracurricular activities, committees, and other faculty tasks?
   • Will you be available outside of the school day and classroom?
   • Will you be willing to take risks?
   • Will you develop your own curriculum?

FURTHER READING

Carlson, J., & Thorpe, C. (1984). Communication: Learning to give and take. *The growing teacher: How to become the teacher you've always wanted to be.* Upper Saddle River, NJ: Merrill/Prentice Hall.

Conoley, J. (1989). Professional communication and collaboration among educators. In Reynolds, M. (Ed.), *Knowledge base for the beginning teacher.* New York: Pergamon Press.

Copeland, W. (1978). Processes mediating the relationship between cooperating teacher behavior and student-teacher classroom performance. *Journal of Educational Psychology, 70,* 95–100.

Doll, R. (1992). The planning process. *Curriculum improvement: Decision making and process.* Boston: Allyn & Bacon.

Hunter, M. (1976). *Teach more–Faster.* El Segundo, CA: TIP Publications.

Johnson, D. (1993). *Reaching out.* Boston, MA: Allyn & Bacon.

Johnson, R., & Johnson, D. (1991). *Joining together.* Upper Saddle River, NJ: Merrill/Prentice Hall.

Chapter Sixteen

IT'S NOT WHAT YOU SAID;
IT'S HOW YOU SAID IT!

SETTING

High School Sophomore English Class

FOCUS QUESTIONS

When reading this case, consider the following questions:

- How do tone of voice and inflection affect how a teacher's words in the classroom are interpreted?
- Can a teacher's choice of words and use of language be a subtle form of discrimination?

George was an extremely intelligent man. His background in literature and writing was extensive, and he brought to his education classes a deep commitment to the profession that inspired the other teachers-to-be in our department. His student teaching assignment was teaching sophomore English in a working class suburban area.

George would be working with Mike, a veteran teacher whose focus was encouraging his students to do their best. I had worked with Mike before and was comfortable with his views of student teaching. I ask all of my student teachers and cooperating teachers to meet and interview each other to determine their expectations for this experience and to begin to establish a comfortable relationship. George reported that he and Mike had outlined a plan for the semester: George would focus on teaching process writing with emphasis on organizational skills. Later, he would add in literature by teaching a novel and perhaps some poetry.

I expressed to George and to all of the students during our initial meeting the importance of effective interaction with the classroom teacher. I reminded them that the cooperating teacher would still be "the teacher of record" and ultimately responsible for the students. "I will be observing your growth as a teacher," I concluded. "Let me know when you are ready for me to come to watch you teach, and keep in mind that I don't expect you to immediately be handling all the classes or even one entire class. Start with one component of a class, we'll discuss how that goes, and then you can begin to take on more responsibility."

Three days later I got a call from George. When I asked him what was up, he told me that he was concerned that his cooperating teacher was not letting him do what was expected for a student teacher. When I pressed him for details, George said that he was ready to take over the writing unit that was underway in his classes, but that Mike wouldn't let him. I reminded George that he and his cooperating teacher needed to work out a mutually agreeable schedule and pointed out that he had been in the classroom for only three days. "I'm not so sure that Mike has my best interests at heart," George commented. At this point, I told George that I would connect with Mike and that I'd be out the next day so that all three of us could sit down and discuss the situation. When I called Mike later that day, he quickly agreed to a meeting, saying that he wasn't sure George was ready to handle an entire lesson, let alone all the classes.

"I believe that all beginning teachers can leave student teaching ready to meet the challenges of the classroom," Mike added. "He'll get to teach, but I want George to observe some more first. He seems to talk above the kids a bit; his humor is so cerebral that the kids don't always get what he is saying. He's been doing attendance and announcements, so he is communicating with the students. I want him to continue to watch these kids and get a better perspective of their world, so that when he teaches, he can connect the information to their lives."

"Let's talk about that during our meeting tomorrow," I suggested.

When the three of us met during Mike's prep period the next day, I suggested that we lay out an explicit timetable and plan for George's student teaching. Mike offered to have George start with one class next week and said that he would like George to initially follow the objectives and lesson plan that had been prepared;

in subsequent weeks, George could begin to plan and implement his own lessons. Mike asked for George's observations about the students he would be teaching.

"Well, these kids really do not seem very motivated. The assignments that I have read are pretty simplistic. I would like to push them to a deeper level of writing."

"That's a good thought," Mike responded. "But many of these kids come from families that don't read, not even a newspaper. Writing is not a high priority. With the downsizing at many of the local plants, lots of these kids are worried about Mom or Dad—or both parents—getting laid off. Some kids in our classes are homeless because of financial difficulties. These are good kids, but you need to understand where they are coming from. My goal is to connect the lessons with the students' lives, so that writing well or reading and understanding good literature is meaningful to them or provides them a way to understand themselves and life a bit better."

As I walked out of the building, George accompanied me. He mentioned that he felt Mike didn't have high enough expectations for the students in his classes.

"I expect the students to focus on their work and to produce high quality writing. If I don't expect that from them, they will never rise to that level," George added.

I thought about the meeting later that night and decided that both Mike and George had valid points. Mike saw the need to make the learning relevant and connected to the students' lives; George wanted to encourage them to achieve by having high expectations. If these two ideas could be blended into George's teaching, he would have a successful experience. If not, there were rocky times ahead.

A week later I stopped out to watch George as he implemented the lesson that Mike had given him to teach. Pensive and philosophical in his description of the task, George took quite a while to explain to the students that he wanted them to write a one-paragraph description of a feeling—an emotion that they had experienced. The objective was to integrate more descriptive language into their writing, and George read the students an example that he had completed. His slow, theatrical delivery produced giggles from some of the girls in the class. Still, he got the students writing and then put them into groups to exchange and peer-edit their classmate's work.

In our post-conference discussion, I commented that George had successfully engaged the students in their writing, and Mike added that most students were on-task throughout the lesson. I asked George if he felt the pace of the lesson had been comfortable. When he said that he hadn't really considered the pace, I suggested that perhaps he needed to shorten his instructions and explain the task a bit more quickly so he wouldn't lose students' attention.

"Did you mention to the kids WHY you were having them do this assignment?" Mike asked.

Again, George stated that he hadn't thought to do that. We talked about the importance of making the learning relevant to the students' lives, and Mike gave an example that he often used.

"I will write the word *stuff* on the board and ask the kids what this means. We then generate a list of other words that could be substituted for the word *stuff*. This idea came to me from an old George Carlin comedy bit. If I talk for a few minutes using *stuff* as about every other word, the kids really get the point. I then tell them that their writing and speaking is more direct and to the point if they use variety and descriptive language."

George acknowledged that he had never considered giving a reason for the assignment. "I just figured that the kids are here to learn, and they will be graded on the assignment, so naturally they will want to do their best."

"Not all kids come from a background where grades are important," Mike commented. "We need to give them a reason to be involved, to create excitement and interest, or these kids will say 'why bother?'"

The three of us determined that George was going to work on stating the purpose of his lessons to the class and to pick up the pace when giving instructions to the class. Mike offered to help George write his objectives in clear, student-focused terms as George began to create his own lessons for the next week. I breathed a sign of relief as they set up a time to meet each day to review George's plans and collaborate on the lessons.

Two weeks later I headed out to George's class to observe him again. His first class went well, although there still was an academic, college-like quality to George's conversations with his students. His vague musings about the value of writing still didn't clarify the specific objective and purpose of the lesson. While George taught the second-period class, Mike and I had a chance to chat.

"I'm not sure about George," Mike began. "His interactions with students often seem to upset the kids. Several students have complained about his teaching, saying that they feel stupid and put down by George's approach and use of 'big words'. The kids have told me that they think George feels he is very much 'above' the students in his classes and that they are often confused by what he says."

"It's not uncommon for students to prefer their regular teacher and be somewhat disconcerted by the seeming intrusion of a newcomer in the classroom," I said. "Let's talk to George about what you have told me and give him some more time to connect with the students."

When George and I met later that day, I shared with him my observations that his lesson had indeed been better paced. I also read back to him the comments he had made at the beginning of the lesson and asked for his reaction.

"Well, I guess I don't have the student vernacular down yet," George replied.

Mike and I also mentioned the student reactions to George's language choice.

"I want to be a role model for my students," George replied. "I do not think that using vocabulary that stretches students' thinking is a problem."

"But if a student never feels connected to what is being said, or is continually unclear about the lesson or your perspective due to your language choice, that student might indeed feel put down or uninterested in a lesson that she doesn't understand," I replied.

George thought for a moment and then said that he hadn't thought of it from that angle. He replied that he had been trying to set a standard for his students, but he agreed to think more carefully about his word choice and language.

"Try to be brief, exact, and to the point when you talk with students," I suggested. "This may help students connect with your lessons more effectively."

I made a point of returning to observe George the next week. George told me that he had been thinking a lot about our last conversation, and that he was rethinking the role of the teacher in the classroom. He mentioned that his philosophy had always been to bring students to a higher level of learning and appreciation for literature and writing, but that he needed to work on the basics first. He mentioned that he was concerned that students were being allowed to "run to Mike with complaints," but he realized he needed to modify his approach. George said he had worked on softening his tone and using a less academic approach when teaching. He also remarked that perhaps he was better suited to teaching the advanced classes because he had so much to offer that these average kids didn't appreciate. I told George that teachers couldn't just focus on high achievers, but that schools were there to meet the needs of all students. I reminded him of our discussions about integration, and he agreed that heterogeneous grouping had some advantages. Still, I wondered if he had a realistic picture of the classroom he would most likely be assigned to next year.

The next week, prior to my visit to George's classroom, I received a phone call from Mike. He was very concerned about an incident that had occurred in the classroom. At this point, George had been in the school four weeks. Mike stated that George had told a particular student, "Your grades are so bad at this point that there is no way you can pass." Mike's point was that no student's grades should be set in stone after only four weeks, and he wondered what George considered the purpose of education. He added that the school counselor had heard of this incident and asked to meet with us because of the impact of George's statement on this struggling student.

When I met George the next day before our appointment with the counselor, he expressed concern about how his student teaching experience was progressing. "I expected to be very successful—and now I am being called on the carpet for being honest with a student about the quality of work he was producing."

"Let's hear the counselor's side," I suggested. "It's helpful to get other points of view before jumping to any conclusions."

The school counselor, Mary Lattimer, reiterated Mike's comments about making school relevant for all students. She asked George about his philosophy of education, and George stated that he had high expectations for students, that he believed that all students could and should aspire to thoughtful, in-depth writing and analysis of literature. The counselor then asked George about his background.

"I received my undergraduate degree in English and have worked for a few years as an editor for a small publication. I studied British literature in England for a summer before I began my teacher preparation program here at the university," George explained.

"Well, perhaps you need to get around the school a bit more, see some of the afterschool activities, drive through the neighborhood. These kids can meet your expectations, but not until they see the rationale behind what you are expecting. I would also caution you, as the student you spoke to is a student of color, that you need to be careful that you are not labeling these individuals as failures because of their race or culture. You could find yourself in the middle of a lawsuit as a teacher if you do not provide opportunities for all of the students in your classroom to be successful. That is discriminatory."

George looked stricken. As we left the counselor's office, he said that he had never considered the student's race when he made the comment. "I just wanted him to know the results of his efforts and the ramifications of his lack of responsibility as a student. I didn't mean to imply that he personally was a failure."

After a few moments, I asked George, "Why do you want to become a teacher?"

"I love great books and good writing," he answered. "I know a lot about literature and what encompasses effective writing, and I want to pass that knowledge on to my students. I can give them so much!"

"But teaching isn't just about what *you* give—it's about what the students get and what they need," I countered. "You need to consider how you, as a teacher, affect their lives."

"I see your point," George said thoughtfully, "and I can do that. I just needed to have my eyes opened. I'll focus even more on incorporating student perspectives into my lessons."

I told George that student teaching was about learning how to be an effective teacher and that he had been given an opportunity to make some positive changes that would enhance his abilities. Mike suggested shifting to a team-teaching approach for the next week so he could model some specific behaviors for George to emulate, and this plan was put into place.

Another week passed, and after an observation, Mike and I agreed that George had been making progress. George commented that he had made an "apocalyptic shift" in his views of the classroom and was trying to communicate more effectively with the students. "I learned a lot from team-teaching with Mike," George said. "I'm ready to try it on my own again." We concluded our discussion by completing and signing observational records that indicated that George was progressing positively toward the goals we had established, and everyone seemed comfortable with the outcome.

But the situation was still far from perfect. Mike called me a few days later, concerned that after all of our conversations, another incident had occurred. It seems that two girls were extremely upset and had also gone to the counselor because of the reaction they got from George when they asked for a change of seating. After a few questions, Mike agreed that while he could not know exactly what had transpired because he had been out of the room at the time, he was worried about the students' growing hostility and frustration with George's teaching. Mike said that he had discussed this incident with George, and George's comment that "the immaturity of the students was a key issue in this situation," was what prompted his phone call to me.

When I asked Mike if he thought George could progress enough to be successful in the classroom, Mike replied, "I know that no teacher is perfect. I certainly am still learning, and I really believe that all educators can grow and improve in their effectiveness—that no one is a 'hopeless case'. George is continuing to implement the things we tell him, but I am always surprised about the issues I have to discuss with him. He doesn't seem to relate to these kids on a personal level. I don't know if he can be successful. I suppose it depends on what you mean by success. He still seems too distant, so imperial, as he leads the class. I know that I would not want him teaching my own children because I am not sure that he likes kids, and that is a basic component to being a good teacher."

Mike then went on to ask if he could reduce George's placement so the student teaching would be finished after only 9 or 10 weeks in the classroom. Mike wanted to get back into his classroom as the sole teacher before he lost kids who dropped out or cut classes. I asked Mike to let me check on some options through the university and said that I would get back to him.

I then called George and discussed the situation with him. George said that the two girls didn't like the seating arrangement and had asked to sit by each other. He said he refused their request, and they had blown the situation out of proportion. By having a forum (Mike) to go to with complaints, George did not think the students took him seriously as a teacher.

I brought up George's need to assess the way he talked to the students, suggesting that the tone of voice he used with the girls might have been the problem. George's irritation was clear as he responded, "I cannot change who I am!! The childishness of these young adults amazes me. Just the other day, I was explaining how they need to use the computer, and I told them that it was easy, that even a second grader could do it, and Mike chastised me afterward for putting the kids down by my reference that 'grade-schoolers' could handle the task. I expect these students to act like adults, and I think that coddling them is not the way to get them to learn! They aren't babies. They need to take school more seriously so they don't waste their time—or mine!"

Realizing that George was obviously not able to see things from the same perspective as his cooperating teacher, I mentioned Mike's suggestion about shortening student teaching and asked George for his reaction. George was all for cutting his student teaching down to 10 weeks. He suggested that he could learn a lot by observing other teachers, or that perhaps he could work in an advanced-placement class. I told George that I did not favor shortening his student teaching experience. "You need to develop the ability to work with a wide range of students," I told him. "You can describe an optimum situation and the theory of effective instruction, but you have to be able to live it." I told George that if his cooperating teacher was no longer supportive of George's work in the classroom, then we needed to change his placement. I suggested that George complete the rest of his student teaching in another setting, and he reluctantly agreed, again asking to work with advanced students.

Next week was spring break, and the fact that there would be seven more weeks after that for George to work in another placement made my decision somewhat more acceptable. I suggested to George that he sign up for an interpersonal communication course at our weekend college before he went to his second placement to heighten his awareness of the effect of vocal tone and language choice on conversations between individuals. I wanted George to have success in his student teaching, so I decided I would try and connect him with an AP teacher in an upper middle-class suburban school. I wondered if this was the right direction to take with George. He had done so well in his academic work as a preservice teacher. Why did he have such difficulty connecting with his students? Was there some way that we could have identified this problem earlier? I wondered whether George *could* be successful, and I agonized over this situation. The ultimate question, still to be determined was: Should George be certified to teach?

 ## POINTS TO PONDER

1. What responsibility does a teacher preparation program have to identify students who might not be effective teachers? What process would you suggest for making such a decision?

2. Should student teachers be placed in settings where they feel they are most likely to succeed (as in an advanced placement course for George)? Or should they have a more typical placement?

3. What are the realities of inclusion? How will you plan lessons that meet the needs of a wide range of learners within one class? How will you interact with students from differing ability levels and diverse backgrounds?

4. Tape-record your voice during a conversation with a friend. Does your tone of voice and word choice seem appropriate for classroom interactions? If not, how will you modify and adjust your speech to create an environment where students feel accepted?

5. Can all students be held to the same standards? If you expect less from some students, is that discrimination? Can you realistically expect the same high levels of learning from all students?

6. What is the purpose of evaluating students? Should grading policies and practices be so rigid that students who do poorly early on have no chance to redeem themselves?

FURTHER READING

Adler, R., Rosenfeld, L., & Towne, N. (1989). *Interplay: The process of interpersonal communication.* Chicago: Holt, Rinehart & Winston.

Brophy, J. (1979). Teacher behavior and its effects. *Journal of Educational Psychology, 71*(6), 733–750.

Good, T. (1988). Teacher expectations. In D. Berliner & B. Rosenshine (Eds.), *Talks to teachers.* New York: Random House.

Reed, S., & Sautter, R. C. (June, 1990). Children of poverty: The status of 12 million young Americans. *Phi Delta Kappan, 71*, 1–4.

Tauber, R., & Mester, C. (1994). *Acting lessons for teachers.* Westport, CT: Praeger.

Samorar, L., Porter, R., & Nemi, J. (1981). *Understanding intercultural communication.* Belmont, CA: Wadsworth.

Wentz, P., & Yarling, J. (1994). *Student teaching casebook for supervising teachers and teaching interns.* Upper Saddle River, NJ: Merrill/Prentice Hall.

Wiggins, G. (1991). Standards not standardization. *Educational Leadership, 48*(5), 18–25.

Chapter Seventeen

ON MY OWN: SINK OR SWIM?

SETTING

High School Social Studies

FOCUS QUESTIONS

When reading this case, consider the following questions:

- How important is it to interact with other teachers during your student teaching experience?
- Should your cooperating teacher be your only contact person?

When I first met with Darlene Reese, Ryan's cooperating teacher, I commented on the many plaques and trophies displayed around the classroom.

"I've been the coach for the Current Events Competition and the Quiz Bowl for a number of years, and we've been very successful," she commented.

"Well, you must be very dedicated to produce such positive results, " I replied. Returning to the purpose of our meeting, I asked, "What would your timeline be for Ryan as he takes on the teaching responsibilities in your classes?"

"Ryan can determine that for himself. He's been observing my classes off and on during the past semester, and I feel very comfortable with his abilities. He mentioned that he might want to begin with the second-hour American History class and then add the first-hour class. He could pick up the three sections of World History after that."

"Sounds like a good approach," I agreed. "The University does urge the students to work into their experience gradually."

"Well, I think Ryan can determine his schedule—he's really very good in the classroom. When he was here observing last week, I had to run to the office, and he handled the class discussion while I was gone."

"Great! " I agreed that Ryan was very confident and knowledgeable. I briefly went over the handbook that we provided as a resource for cooperating teachers, as it outlined the approach and activities that the university prescribed for student teachers. "Do you have a specific time available when you and Ryan can meet each day to talk about his lessons and discuss any concerns he might have?" I inquired.

"We'll have to sit down and take a look at my schedule," Darlene said. "Both of my academic teams are gearing up for our competitive season, so I may be pretty busy after school."

"Using your prep time or meeting over lunch has been a way that many student teachers and cooperating teachers get together. We feel it is very important that the two of you communicate on a regular basis so that you are both aware of the other's expectations."

"We'll work something out," Darlene said as she stood up. "Thanks for coming out. I have to go meet my team captains now, so you'll have to excuse me."

As I walked out of the high school, I felt slightly uneasy. I hoped that Darlene would not be too busy to provide Ryan with the support and mentoring he needed. When I met with my student teachers in our seminar later that day, I pointed out that two or three students were placed at each site.

"You will want to connect with your peers outside of our seminar sessions. I will be out to observe you about every other week, and we have five seminars scheduled to discuss common issues and concerns. It will be helpful to spend some time with the other student teachers in your building to share ideas and stories. You might meet over lunch or after school for pizza—whatever. Developing collegial relationships is very important for teachers; we can't isolate ourselves in the classroom and expect that we can deal with everything on our own. That is also why the university asks that you interview the people who provide support services to teachers in your building—to get you out and about in the school community. This assignment is described in your student teaching guide, as well as the request for weekly reflection. I will want to see your lesson plans when I visit you and to look over your journal. I want us to be able to connect via several mediums, so don't hesitate to call or e-mail me if you have any concerns."

As the students were leaving, I asked Ryan if he was aware of the heavy involvement Darlene had with the Quiz Bowl and Current Events Teams.

"Oh yes, that's why I want to work with her. She has a great reputation. She said that I can help with the team practices; she seems pretty comfortable with my teaching."

"Well, just don't take on too much at once, Ryan," I cautioned. "You have had some experience in teaching at the camps you've worked at during the summer, but the school environment can be quite different. Take it slow and be sure you are comfortable with one class before you take on another or add extra duties."

Ryan smiled,"I want to get the most out of this experience that I can. I plan to hit the ground running!"

Two weeks later, I made my first visit to Ryan's school, and Darlene and I watched Ryan lead a lively discussion regarding state's rights and the Civil War. Afterwards Darlene said that she was very pleased with Ryan's teaching and that she'd be available later if I had any questions. With that, she left, and I asked Ryan to describe what he'd been doing so far.

"I observed for the first day, but I was just itching to get in front of the class, so Darlene let me take over the second-hour American History class on the second day. I followed her lesson plan for a couple of days, but she said I could develop my own lesson, based on her curriculum outline, after that. What did you think?"

I complemented Ryan on the way he had tied the issue of state's rights into the students' lives by asking them to identify issues where they felt they were "at odds" with another group. We discussed his lesson plans, and I pointed out that Ryan was indeed well organized and prepared.

"Do you have your journal for me to see?" I asked next.

"Well, to be honest, when I began to plan my own lessons, I needed so much time for that, I just didn't get to the journal. I will next week though."

"What kind of schedule do you and Darlene have for conferring about your day?"

"We have hall duty fifth hour, and we stand by the door to check for student passes. We've been discussing the day and my lesson plans then."

"Does this seem to work?" I inquired.

"Well, sometimes we need to redirect a lot of students so we often get interrupted. But Darlene said she'd tell me if there was anything wrong with what I was doing. So far, she's been very complimentary."

I located Darlene in the library, working with members of her quiz bowl team. "I was wondering if you could squeeze in some time for conferring with Ryan about his teaching in a more relaxed setting, rather than during hall duty," I began.

"Well, he's doing fine, so we really don't have much to talk about," Darlene interjected. "I told Ryan when he asked to student teach with me that my schedule was jam-packed and that he'd be on his own a lot. He is fine with this, and so am I. Ryan is very effective in the classroom. He just needs time to hone his skills—and he's certainly getting that in my classroom! If I had any concerns, I would be in the classroom more, but Ryan is able to handle things. He is getting a much more realistic view of the life of a teacher by doing it all. I believe he will be much better prepared than some of your student teachers who teach only one or two classes. That isn't the reality of teaching."

I agreed that Ryan was capable but added, "Sometimes a student teacher begins strong, but halfway through the semester, begins to have questions about their teaching. Ryan is a strong beginning teacher, but there is much more he could explore and develop in his teaching." I pointed out that he seemed to be ignoring several students in the discussion and that he needed to involve all of the class. I was especially concerned because in one class the group Ryan ignored was primarily African American males, and in the other, it was a group of kids in the back row who seemed to be having their own private conversation. "Ryan has good lesson plans and he is developing his skills in leading a discussion, but he needs to consider other areas," I concluded.

"I am sure that he will find a way to deal with these issues," Darlene said. "I will mention your comments to him and suggest that he think about how he wants to deal with this. I am sure Ryan will consider the issue and come to a conclusion—and will be a better teacher for solving the problem himself!"

When I left the building after conversing with my other student teachers, it was clear that Ryan was not connecting with the other two young people teaching in the school. I worried that Ryan was not getting the support he needed. I know that good teachers can be empowered to facilitate their own professional development, but I was not convinced that Ryan could do this in isolation. He was adamant that he was "doing fine" and "loving" the experience, so I decided not to press the issue of Darlene's lack of involvement with her student teacher.

The semester progressed, and I tried to meet with Ryan as often as I could. He sometimes seemed tired and would mention that he had helped with quiz bowl mock competitions after school and with weekend meets. However, his lessons were well planned, he began to use more cooperative learning, and he seemed eager to implement the suggestions I made. He insisted that he was gaining a lot of valuable experience, and while he appreciated my comments, he required no change in the interaction Darlene was providing, nor did he want to chat with his colleagues.

"It feels good to know that I can handle all of the aspects of teaching," he said.

At our full-group meeting following the semester of student teaching, many of the student teachers shared stories of the bond they had developed with their cooperating teacher. When asked to share a highlight from his experience, Ryan said, "I know that I can handle myself in the classroom—I was given the chance to do it all—and I succeeded. That is, to me, a great feeling, and a strong validation of my skills."

I had been concerned about Ryan's lack of support, but he seemed very comfortable with it. Perhaps I had been guilty of trying to force one model of student teaching onto this situation when Ryan and Darlene were more comfortable with their own approach. Did individuals have a need for different student teaching models, just as students require different teaching to support their learning styles? Ryan received a glowing evaluation from Darlene, and he went on to teach in a small suburban middle school. Case closed—or at least, so I thought.

I liked to do follow-up interviews with former student teachers who are now teaching, so I met with Ryan for lunch in November to discuss how he felt his student teaching had prepared him for his new job.

"One of the things I really love about this school is the comradery among the staff," was Ryan's first comment. "I work on the seventh-grade team, and we get together for planning and really are able to 'connect' with all our lessons. It's not quite at the level of true interdisciplinary planning, but that's the direction we're moving. It's really fun to bounce ideas off of each other."

"This kind of collegial interaction is quite different from that of your student teaching experience," I stated. "How do you think your student teaching would have been affected if you'd had more interaction from your cooperating teacher and other teachers?"

Ryan thought for a while. "I really needed to prove to myself that I could teach, and I did that. Darlene rarely observed the classroom after the first few weeks, and our brief conversations during fifth hour never could cover more than just the essential communications that we had to share. Because I worked with her academic teams, I usually ate lunch in my room while working with students, and I spent prep time and after school either planning my lessons or working with students for competition. Darlene had warned me when I asked to work with her that I'd be on my own a lot, that she didn't have much extra time, so I was okay with the way the semester went. I know I gained valuable experiences, but this approach did limit me somewhat."

"Perhaps I should have placed you with another cooperating teacher when I saw the route that you two were taking," I commented.

"I wouldn't have wanted to move. I was comfortable with how Darlene and I divided responsibilities; my self-esteem and confidence went up each day. Still, I wonder what else I might have experienced if I'd had a different relationship with my cooperating teacher. I didn't really have time for much reflection. Because Darlene and I were so involved with preparing the academic team, I rushed through my journals and didn't get a chance to meet most of the support people you asked us to interview."

"I told you I felt your reflections lacked depth," I reminded him, smiling.

"Remember when you commented during an early class that I seemed to ignore certain groups of students? I was embarrassed to say that I felt intimidated by the Black guys and the group that was goofing off, so I tried to avoid them. As the semester went on and I felt more confident and I began to interact with both groups more. As a result, I gained a deeper understanding of the African American perspective of history, I learned to move kids around the room to separate those who were goofing off, and I recognized the need to engage *all* students in the learning with group activities and cooperative lessons. But I always had a sense that I was 'experimenting'. I was so nervous about doing the wrong thing that I avoided some students and missed some opportunities to learn. It would have been nice to talk to someone about how I felt, but like I said, I was embarrassed. I mean, I had taken multicultural education classes and discussed classroom management in my methods course, but I realize now that my background was pretty limited. During the semester, I was so caught up in 'being the teacher', that I just didn't want to talk about those issues—I wanted to handle things myself."

"Ryan, why didn't you talk to me? Your stock answer when I visited was that everything was okay. You could have connected with other educators, including your fellow student teachers, at school. You never mentioned any of these concerns during our seminars or in your journal, either," I stated.

"I know. I knew I was managing to handle everything by myself, so I didn't feel I needed to discuss things. Now that I'm working on a team where the norm is that we talk about *everything*, I have a little different perspective. I wonder, what if I had created a problem with those guys in my class by ignoring them, and then it escalated into something that I couldn't undo later? What would I have done? I certainly didn't have all the answers then, just as I don't now. Talking to other teachers and discussing concerns and issues really broaden the picture. I am beginning to think that I was really very lucky to get through student teaching unscathed, considering I was 'on my own'."

◉ POINTS TO PONDER

1. Do you think the college supervisor should have moved Ryan to another student teaching placement? How would you react if your initial placement didn't seem to be working?

2. Is there a place in the student teaching experience for the "sink or swim" model? Why or why not?

3. What do student teachers gain from interacting with other teachers and student teachers during the student teaching experience?

4. How will you help develop a relationship with your cooperating teacher that enables you to communicate about issues?

5. Describe the activities, responsibilities, and challenges that you would like to undertake during your student teaching experience.

   • How will these enhance your development as a professional educator?
   • Is it necessary to experience all aspects of the teacher role for successful student teaching?

6. What guidance should you expect from the college in the selection of a cooperating teacher?

FURTHER READING

Britzman, D. P. (1991). *Practice makes practice: A critical study of learning to teach.* Albany, NY: State University of New York Press.

Conoley, J. (1989). Professional communication and collaboration among educators. In Renolds, M. (Ed.), *Knowledge base for the beginning teacher.* New York: Pergamon Press.

Ferri, B., & Aglio, M. (1990). *I'm not alone: Teacher talk, teacher buddying.* Mississauga, Ontario: The Peel Board of Education.

Newman, J. M. (1989). *Finding our own way: Teachers exploring their assumptions.* Portsmouth, NH: Heinemann.

Wentz, P., & Yarling, J. (1994). *Student teaching casebook for supervising teachers and teaching interns.* Upper Saddle River, NJ: Merrill/Prentice Hall.

Chapter Eighteen

REFLECTIONS AND CONNECTIONS

SETTING

Fourth Grade

FOCUS QUESTIONS

When reading this case, consider the following questions:

- What expectations does your college or university have regarding reflection during your student teaching?

- How valuable do you think keeping a journal or reflecting on the interactions in the classroom will be for you?

Flipping through the notebooks that contain the thoughts of the student teachers I was working with this semester, I paused again to read Michelle's comments. I always find it interesting that these young people discover so much about teaching by taking the time to think about what is going on in their classrooms. Rather than just react to events, they analyze and consider the possibilities for shaping what occurs in their classroom. This excerpt from Michelle's required journal provides a sample of some of the issues that can come up during this intensive introduction to teaching.

9-11

"Today is Tuesday, the day you watched me work with the kids in the computer lab. We talked for quite a while after this class, and I appreciate your suggestions, Dr. J., I must have seemed a bit down when we spoke—it was nice of you to make that follow-up call to see how I was doing that night. I have to admit, even though I am just 'helping' at this point, I am very nervous. I know we're supposed to reflect on the day's events each week in this thing—I haven't done that so far. Life as a student teacher is so busy, so I haven't made this writing a priority. It's just that the daily events—learning students' names, doing attendance, helping with lessons—seems a bit overwhelming. The kids are so energetic—I hope I can control them.

"I did all of the preliminary stuff you asked us to complete the first few weeks. I've read the faculty handbook and the school policy. Mr. Hasselford and I have set up when I'll take over—but we're going to do this gradually. I am trying to get ahead on some planning for when I do teach—that seems more important right now. I have to admit, I was surprised when you asked to see my journal during your visit today, but what you said makes sense—that if I spend a few moments writing down my thoughts and concerns, I will take more time to consider how to deal with these issues, rather than just reacting and then moving on. So, I'll try to keep my journal up to date."

9-18

"Today I taught a lesson on the geography of the Northeast, and the kids seemed so bored. I called on individuals to read the social studies text, and then I explained it. Some of them really struggled with the text. Mr. H. said I was spoon-feeding them too much. So tomorrow I am going to put them into groups and let them answer questions together rather than give them the answers. This ought to involve the students in the learning a bit more and enable some of the better readers to help out those who have difficulty, without the whole class watching. I feel bad when I see those glazed looks on their faces. I need to learn how to be more interesting."

10-3

"I have been here three weeks already, and time seems to be flying by. I have noticed, as you said, that things feel more comfortable as I get more experience. I am doing more and more of the teaching each day. One interesting thing—I have been trying to get the children to predict what might be coming next in the stories we are reading. Sometimes they get really upset and say that this spoils the story when they have heard someone else tell them the ending. I find myself getting irritated at this often-repeated complaint. When I tried to explain to the students that I wanted them to stretch their thinking and use the author's clues to speculate on what might be the next event in the story, they had a better suggestion. Carrie called out, "Why can't we just write down what we think and then read the whole thing and afterwards see if what we wrote really happened?" I was upset that I hadn't been able to think of this solution! Of course this worked very well, and the children liked the mystery of disclosing whose prediction came closest to the actual storyline. I am amazed that something so simple didn't cross my mind until the students suggested it! Maybe I should listen to them more often."

10-15

"I know that I tend to speak too fast. I am trying to work on this. My cooperating teacher reminded me that I need to model correct usage, but I know I say *ya* for *you* and *ta* for *to* and things like *don't cha* for *don't you*. Maybe I do this because I speak too rapidly. I don't want to be so formal that I distance myself from the kids, but I do know that sometimes I have to repeat myself because I rattle off directions too rapidly. When you talked about 'ongoing development' Dr. J., I guess that this is an area that I will need to focus on. I definitely want the children to know the difference between speaking casually and speaking formally. I hear street English all the time in the classroom, and I know that for many of the students, it is their natural style of conversation. What I need to do is develop a lesson that lets them use their natural language and then translate that into different styles. We could do a brief story and then write the same thing as a newspaper article and then as a formal report. By having the kids read these out loud, they would hear the difference. Maybe I would have to write examples the first time, but I am sure that they could do this themselves after we went through it together! Hey—I guess I have just developed another lesson!"

10-25

"We're going to have a test in math tomorrow over adding and subtracting three-digit numbers. One boy asked me, 'What happens if I can't get the test done during class?' I was faced with making a decision: Do I give them more time? Do we finish this tomorrow? We have to go to Physical Education afterwards, and this limits the time for the test . . . So I told them I would check with Mr. Hasselford during lunch and let them know later. After I said this, I realized how often those words come out of my mouth, 'I'll check with Mr. H.'. Maybe this makes me seem very insecure about my decisions. But I like the fact that this provides a delaying tactic, and it gives me time to think about what I want to do. When I have my own classroom,

I'll probably say, 'Let me think about that and we'll decide tomorrow'. This way, I won't make any rash decisions that will come back to haunt me later!"

10-30

"Today I had a hard time getting the students to settle down. How long do you give students to calm down and pay attention? How long should I wait? It seems like I could stand in front of the class in silence for the whole day! Mr. H. told me that one time he laid down on the floor to see if anyone would notice, and it still took them 10 minutes to calm down and wonder if something was wrong!

How much do I ignore? How much should I expect? I am not sure what behaviors I should ignore and which ones I should reprimand them for! I always address the big problems—someone pushing or out of their seat for no apparent reason—but what about all the little things they do? Should I ignore these things and hope they go away? Getting them to focus on the key points of a lesson rather than just chit-chat seems to be my biggest challenge. I want these kids to be able to discuss what we're learning in social studies and literature, but what about students who ask questions or make comments that don't have anything to do with the book? I don't want to squash their natural enthusiasm, but when they talk, they get off on tangents so easily. I could give them questions to answer on a worksheet, but I'd rather they share their ideas. Maybe I could have them write things down and then talk . . . I might give that a try."

11-5

"Well, using the focus questions before class discussion is working pretty well! As you said when you were here the other day, the children are on task. You also pointed out with your diagram of who was talking to whom, that I do call on the guys more. Three or four boys tend to dominate the conversation. I need to call on specific people more often, like you suggested. All of the kids have answers written down, because I collect them, but I need to encourage some of the girls to speak up and share their ideas out loud. I think that I will draw names out of a hat tomorrow to get a more random approach."

11-8

"Today I decided to add a journal assignment to our lesson, but I gave the journal topic without giving much description. My cooperating teacher does not use journals, but I really think that they need to write. They looked at the cover of the book, *Number the Stars* and wrote a journal entry about what the picture might indicate that the story could be about. We talked about power and leadership and what we would do if a leader used his position to hurt people. I asked if anyone knew about Hitler, and I got a few comments. Although there was some confusion at first, the kids settled down and wrote some interesting things. I discovered that I have several Jewish children (they commented on the Star of David), and many kids who watch too much television! I am going to develop a list of story starters that relate to subjects we are studying in school and current event items for the class to respond to in journals. I am still not sure if they should write every week or every day and whether I should grade the journals.

"After this lesson, my cooperating teacher said that one of the boys was acting up in the back. I didn't even notice him! I let them to sit together to share a book, and I should have put Mark next to someone else, not Brian. Why do I miss some of the off-task behavior that experienced teachers see? I feel that I am progressing and getting the students to focus more. I move around the room and give them my best "let's-get-with-it" look. Still, not everyone is involved in the learning.

"I teach everything by myself now, but having Mr. H. observe me made me nervous today."

11-20

"A concern I have is that there is one student who is very loud and who could be a problem. Josh didn't turn in the journal writing assignment yesterday (I am using them more frequently now—with good results!). I told him what his grade would be if he didn't do it—I am giving points for each journal assignment. He brought in a brief paragraph today, and I took 8 points off for its being late. This lowered his average grade and will give him a D for the midterm. He is a bright little guy, but he just doesn't do the work. So does the grade reflect his effort or his actual work? Shanna gets everything done on time, but her work is very poor, yet Josh is getting a lower grade. I am not sure I buy this letter grade system. I need to figure out a better method. The book you suggested about writing work-shops is in the faculty development library here at school; I'll check it out and see if it offers any ideas."

11-26

"A few days off felt great! I am skimming through Atwell's book. She suggests that portfolios be used to look at the progress and improvement of writing over time. I like this idea, but I can't use it now, because I have to generate grades for Mr. H.'s grade book. I think I'll just use the point system (taking so much off for incomplete sentences, etc.) that Mr. H. uses.

"I just turned on the television and heard someone say that it wasn't the good things that happened in our lives that molded us into who were, but the bad times, the rough parts of our lives that shape us. He was talking about big disaster, but it seemed to relate to me. I am not enjoying student teaching in the way that I expected. But, almost every job that I've had I was uncomfortable with at the beginning. Right now, I do not feel confident in this job. I love teaching and the kids, but I still feel there is so much I don't know! What will I do when I don't have someone like Mr. H. or you to talk to? Thinking about what this guy said on the TV, I have to say that every day I am faced with something that I have to deal with and make a decision about. As a result, I learn something new every day. I realize that this is a good thing for me, even if it's hard. It is a chance for me to grow and to become a stronger and more confident person."

12-1

"Something happened today that was really neat. We were doing a science experiment, and I was taking students through the process step by step. I was concerned that I was doing too much, so I let the students go ahead and work on their own. One girl said, 'I liked it better when you helped us.' So I went back and let those students who wanted me to lead them to join me and let those who wanted to go on their own to do so. One student said, 'I really like it when you take it one step at a time'. Just like we learned in my education classes, this points out the need to address individual learning styles. My split-second decision had been a good one. It felt great to know that I had hit upon something that worked! I don't like leaving this to chance, though. I need to find out more about each of these kids and see what I can do to help them learn in a way that is easier for them."

12-8

"I graded the student projects for *Number the Stars* today. I wanted to make positive comments on all of them, and then I realized that I hadn't created any system for what was going to determine the grade. I thought it would be great for the kids to come up with creative projects that depicted a scene from the book. Some were great—some were terrible. But I wasn't sure if I was grading the artistic element or the idea they portrayed. I certainly never told the class how I would grade these things. Why didn't I create a rubric so that the kids (and I) would know up front what was expected? So I am back to that grade issue again. Do I have to give a specific grade for everything they do? How do I determine the quarter grades for the report cards? This is the first year these kids get a letter grade, in first to third grade, they get an S (satisfactory) or an N (needs improvement). How do I create a system that is fair? Mr. H. told me the process he uses, but I don't like the idea of points off for spelling errors and grammar mistakes. I want to encourage them to write and express their ideas. Can you really compare and label their work?"

12-14

"I only have two weeks left of teaching here. Mr. H and I are team-teaching now so that it will be easier for him when I leave. It is comfortable to work with him now that I feel more confident about my teaching. The children are excited about the upcoming winter break and are often loud and disruptive. It doesn't unnerve me now the way it did in the beginning, although I still struggle to get them focused. I am trying to come up with nonreligious holiday projects and ideas. You were there when we were doing graphing in math yesterday, and one of the graphs showed the results of a class bake sale. When the students asked if they could have a bake sale, and Mr. H. said he thought that would be a good project to undertake before the holidays, I was a bit apprehensive. Your comments about how this could involve so many of the math skills we have been learning really helped me take charge of this activity.

"So, to begin with, we are surveying the other classes to find out what are their favorite kinds of cookies; then we are going to select the top three kinds of cookies to bake. We've got permission to use the school cafeteria after lunch, and several parents have responded to our requests for help. This seems a bit over-whelming, but the children are so excited. We've been discussing fractions (looking at recipes) and cost (how much to charge per cookie?) and why some people might prefer peanut butter cookies over chocolate chip. We compiled the results of our surveys and chose our three kinds of cookies; then Mr. H. bought the ingredients. The kids know they have to pay him back from our profits, but they hope to make a little money. The big controversy was what to do with the money we make. We had everyone write down an idea and then read them to the class. Afterwards we voted on one idea—and the money is going to go to the local food shelf to provide food for those who need it over the holidays. (It might be that some of these kids' families will benefit from our work.) In any case, this project has become a very big deal. I would be nervous about doing it myself, but with Mr. H. to help, I feel confident that this is going to be a great learning experience.

"By the way—it was nice to hear your comments on my speaking. I hadn't noticed that I have slowed my pace. I think that I'm not as worried about getting through my lesson as I am about the children's understanding what we're doing."

12-22

"Today was my last day. We had a great week—the cookie sale went very well. The children created signs for advertising, and the principal let them make an announcement over the P.A. system. Baking the cookies got a bit confusing and we burned a panful. But the kids worked well in their teams, and they all completed the specific tasks they were assigned. I came up with the job descriptions, and we ran this like a business. The kids really enjoyed it even though I had to put everyone on dishwashing detail because no one wanted that job! With supervision, things went well, although the first batch that Josh, Tyrone, Mike, and Sara mixed up they put all the ingredients in together and mixed it all at once rather than following directions. The texture was a bit different, but they really read the directions carefully after that! (Mr. H. told the kids that the way different ingredients combined was like a chemistry experiment. The children seemed interested in this approach, so I made a note to look into science and cooking for future science lessons.)

"When all the cookies were baked, we made trayfuls of assorted cookies, and pairs of kids took them to the classrooms. We sold almost all of them, and the class decided to donate the leftover cookies to the faculty lounge for the teachers. After paying back Mr. H., we had $57.00 to donate. The kids really felt good about what they had done, and I know they learned some valuable life skills. Best of all, I feel that after managing that project I can handle most teaching tasks!

"The class made me a card for my last day, and I feel such a mix of emotions. I will miss these energetic little people! I am still nervous because there seems to be so much yet that I don't know—so many decisions in the classroom that I will have to make on my own. Am I really ready for my own classroom?"

POINTS TO PONDER

1. After reading Michelle's reflective writing, what were her early concerns? What did she describe later in her journal? Do you think her journal keeping indicates that she is changing her focus over time? Why or why not?

2. Identify the specific issues and concerns that Michelle mentioned in her journal. Did she deal with these things? How would you handle these issues?

3. Why might writing your thoughts in a journal format be helpful to a beginning teacher?

4. How will you prioritize the use of your time during student teaching? Consider how you will manage to find time to reflect on your work as a teacher.

FURTHER READING

Atwell, N. (1987). *In the middle: Writing, reading and learning with adolescents.* Portsmouth, NH: Boynton/Cook.

Clift, R., Houston, R., & Pugach, M. (Eds.). (1990). *Encouraging reflective practice in education: An analysis of issues and programs.* New York: Teacher College Press.

Grimmett, P., & Erickson, G. (Eds.). (1988). *Reflection in teacher education.* New York: Teachers College Press.

Ross, J. A., & Regan, E. M. (1993). Sharing professional experience: Its impact on professional development. *Teaching and Teacher Education, 9*(1), 91–106.

Russell, T. (1993). Reflection-in-action and the development of professional expertise. *Teacher Education Quarterly, 20*(1), 51–62.

Schon, D. A. (1990). *Educating the reflective practitioner.* San Francisco: Jossey-Bass.

Chapter Nineteen

BEYOND THE CLASSROOM

SETTING

Fifth Grade, Urban School

FOCUS QUESTIONS

When reading this chapter, consider the following questions:

● What do you know about the committees and educational activities that teachers are involved in after school?

● What role will you play in the development of your school community?

Thomas was a patient, understanding young man who enjoyed involving his students in hands-on activities in his classroom. He was more interested in getting the kids involved in the learning than cracking down on minor infractions. As his college supervisor, I observed his classes with delight, as he worked hard to implement cooperative learning strategies and help his students learn to work together to solve problems and resolve differences.

During one of our conferences after I had observed his morning lessons, I remarked to Thomas that I thought he looked a little tired. He replied that he had put in a 14-hour day two days ago and hadn't caught up yet. The extra time was spent preparing for the school's annual learning festival. This event combined a science fair with learning presentations to create a fun celebration. Fifth- and sixth-grade students were required to produce a science project, and other classes put on plays or displayed their art work, writing, and graphs of math lessons. Music was provided, a raffle was held to generate some extra funding, and games and treats were provided to keep the younger students involved. This year a reading corner was being added, complete with a professional storyteller. After hearing about the festival, I commented that this event was a wonderful example of how a school can celebrate learning and give children an opportunity to demonstrate their progress.

While Thomas agreed, he also said that he had no idea when he began his student teaching experience that he would put in so much time beyond his preparation for classroom teaching. I asked him to elaborate, and I discovered that his immersion into the school community involved spending hours and hours after school at meetings and planning sessions. I was concerned that all of this extra work might affect his teaching. After all, he was a beginner and needed more time than experienced teachers to plan and organize lessons. I suggested that he might want to cut back a little on the extracurricular events. Thomas nodded, but added that he felt compelled to participate in many of the meetings because his cooperating teacher was involved and had invited him to come along.

"I know that I am gaining a lot from these activities, but I guess I was a little naive about what the job of teacher entailed," Thomas added. "A lot of time is spent being involved in important decisions that will affect the classroom, but these are often nonpaid events for teachers. No one tells you about these extra hours in your education classes, but I think that if you want to teach well, it is necessary to be involved with more than just your own lessons."

When I asked for more detail regarding these extra duties, he rattled off the various activities that went on in his building after class was dismissed for the day: Parent Teacher Organization meetings; Chess Club, Science Club, library aide meetings, and intramural athletics for the kids; workshops on leadership training and peer evaluation; faculty meetings and subcommittee meetings for teachers; curriculum development committees and the inevitable time spent correcting papers and planning lessons. Thomas added that his cooperating teacher spent an average of five hours a day working outside of the classroom, and that he had realized by the second day of classes that he could not be a full-time teacher without putting in many hours beyond the classroom.

"I spent a lot of time after school helping my students get ready for their science projects. We discussed topics in class, but I helped them find resources in the library and scrounged up posterboard and markers to create visual presentations. There were no Nobel winners in my group, but the kids were excited to show what they had learned. One boy presented a description of how fingerprints were used to track criminals and identify people; another looked at how severe weather develops and created a 'tornado in a jar' so other students could make their own tornado. The night before the festival, my 14-hour day, I stayed to help set up the gym. We had to put up tables for the science displays, hang the artwork and papers, and we also set up the sound system and got the refreshments organized. It was a lot of work, but the kids were so excited the next day to see all of their work displayed that it was worth it. The parents who came for the evening activities were pleased to see evidence of their children's learning. All of the children received comments on their work from a 'review panel' of teachers, and awards were given for creativity and originality so that everyone received some type of ribbon. The top academic prize for the science project was also selected, and the winner will compete at the state science competition. When everything was over and cleaned up, I was tired, but I felt that the whole school was on a 'high' from our celebration of learning."

Thomas and the other student teachers met every other week in a seminar to discuss topics of interest. I suggested that Thomas might want to share some of his experiences with the various faculty meetings and extracurricular work he had been involved with at school. The first group he described was the Faculty Council. He told his fellow student teachers that the team leader from each grade level participated in the Faculty Council. The primary role of this group for the first part of the year was the budget. A Budget Committee, made up of members of the Faculty Council, determined how the money given to the school by the district was spent. "The first meeting I attended focused on one agenda item," Thomas explained. "This topic was meeting conduct. From what I've been told and what I've observed, each grade level team and every specialist feel they have a right to more money for their students. As the money is apportioned by a consensus from the Budget Committee, there are often heated discussions as individuals try to defend their turf. This seems inevitable when there is too little money to go around."

The preservice teachers discussed the effect of budget cutbacks at their schools, but it seemed that the urban schools, with their greater need, felt the financial pinch the most. Thomas continued, "At the budget meetings, an information sheet passed out by the meetings coordinator displayed the approximately $2.71 allocated for each student for the following calendar year. I couldn't believe it! How could you meet the needs of all the kids with $2.71 per child? The art teacher wanted new supplies, there were not enough computers for all the children, and many of the teachers wanted more hands-on science materials. The math series being used by the school was old and outdated, and several classes were short of texts. Some teachers were photocopying math materials to have something to teach. Since this violates copyright law, and because there is also a severe shortage in funds for copier paper, many teachers refused to make copies, yet they felt that kids were falling behind in math because of the shortage of materials. It seemed that were no other options, so it was decided to fund the purchase of a new math series recommended by the Textbook Committee. While this was agreeable to everyone, there was still disappointment that the money would only go so far."

One of the other student teachers asked what math series was being recommended. When Thomas replied, he added that the whole adoption process for looking at new materials, especially textbooks, was lengthy and guided by district policy. "I haven't seen the new series, but it will be in place by next fall," he said, "I hope it has more real-life problems to use. I have a hard time coming up with problems that are connected to my fifth graders' lives, and I would love a text that provided some examples. But I've heard that the Textbook Committee was influenced heavily by one of the back-to-basics, drill-and-practice teachers, so I don't know."

A topic of interest to everyone at the student teacher seminars was substitute teaching and the hiring of teachers. Noting that many of these young people would begin their career working as a sub, I asked Thomas to outline an issue related to this topic that had been discussed at his school.

"The Faculty Council also dealt with the hiring of teachers. Due to the shuffling of teachers because of seniority and resignation, several long-term substitutes had been assigned to classrooms a few days before school began. These teachers often were not prepared for their last-minute appointments. For example, we had a music teacher placed in a third-grade classroom! Often individuals with experience in the upper grades found themselves in kindergarten and first grade. In addition, it usually took about seven to eight weeks to get the regular teacher hired and in place. Parents were upset when this happened in their child's classroom, so the issue spilled over into the Parent-Teacher Organization and the Leadership Council. The Leadership Council exists because our school is an official site-based management school. The council is composed of teachers, other staff, administrators, a couple of parents, and a sixth-grade student representative. Based on a request from several vocal parents at the PTO meetings, the Leadership Council decided to pass this issue of the use of substitutes to the Human Resources Subcommittee. This subset of the Leadership Council is drafting a policy on the hiring of long-term subs for the full council to approve, and then it will be presented to the faculty, principal, the district administrators, and the school board."

One of the student teachers commented that this lengthy process must be frustrating to everyone involved. "Maybe so," Thomas answered, "but at least something is being done, and many individuals will have a say in the final policy."

"But will the policy generate any change?" asked Becky, another student teacher. "It seems like an awful lot of work with no guarantees."

"My cooperating teacher has really been working on this issue. He says that children get confused when they have different teachers to adjust to at the beginning of the year. Some subs just do review work while they wait for the 'real' teacher to be assigned. In addition, establishing clear classroom rules and routines is difficult, and this affects the whole school," Thomas replied. "I think it is important to get involved in the issues that affect the learning of children. Can you imagine being 6-years-old and, after just getting used to school and your teacher, you find a new face behind the teacher's desk?"

Asked what they thought of the extensive bureaucracy that Thomas had described, several students commented that they were so busy getting their lessons planned that they couldn't possibly spend the time on peripheral issues. "It would take too much time to work through the system. I'd rather just focus on my kids," Becky stated. Other students countered that this attitude was what was responsible for the sad shape schools were in. Becky replied, "My primary goal is to help the kids learn, and if I concentrate on that, then I know I can make a difference."

"Sure," Thomas answered, "But what if you don't have enough books, and you're the teacher dumped into a class the day before school starts and then pulled out two months later? Don't you want to let people know how you feel about these things?"

After they had thought about this issue for a while, I mentioned that besides the Faculty Council and Leadership Council, Thomas also had attended several of the regular monthly faculty meetings. He went on to describe some of the topics that had been discussed in these meetings. "The primary issue has been attendance and student behavior rules. To date, there does not seem to be any official policy. It is up to individual teachers to handle student absences and deal with behavior as they see fit. This has been especially frustrating for me as a student teacher. How can a teacher enforce rules that don't officially exist? Many teachers feel they don't have administrative support in enforcing behavior and attendance policies. There is ongoing discussion, but so far, no steps have been taken to generate a plan or policy. It seems as though the Leadership Council might take up this issue, and with a smaller group, the comments and suggestions of the faculty might be shaped into a policy."

Several of the student teachers sighed and shook their heads. One commented that he had more dimensions to his life than just work and questioned if he would really have the time to devote to the activities and processes Thomas described. Another stated that she did not stay at school as long as her cooperating teacher, but that she felt she worked on her lessons more effectively at home. Others mentioned that they liked the idea of getting involved and having some say in school decisions that affected their classroom.

One person wondered if teachers shouldn't be paid for every hour spent at school in meetings held after the regular contract day. Thomas concluded the discussion for us by saying that he had been surprised by all of the unofficial duties that were part of the work of teachers. "None of the teachers I observed were compensated for the meetings and events they attended. Some committee work-time is paid for with a small honorarium, but I didn't hear of this happening too often at my school. I know that some teachers punch a time clock and stay in the building only for the time specified in their contract, but I can't hide in my classroom and pretend that issues like the budget and hiring don't affect me and my teaching. I know that I want to make a difference in the lives of my students—I want to help them learn. No one will tell you that you have to put in extra hours, but if you want to do the job right, it is necessary."

POINTS TO PONDER

1. As a student teacher, how involved do you plan to be in teaching duties that extend beyond the classroom? What are the benefits and drawbacks of your decision?

2. What administrative issues and topics do you feel strongly about? What role do you envision for yourself regarding these issues and the decision-making processes of your future school?

3. How will you respond to invitations or requests from your cooperating teacher or other teachers that you join them in attending after-school meetings?

4. How would you describe your group interaction skills? Consider how you envision your behavior as a participant in the various meetings described in this case.

5. Identify the educational organizations, at the local, state, and national levels that you could participate in to work toward effective change in education.

6. What is the governing structure of the school systems in your area? Compare the differences and discuss how you would fit into such an organizational structure.

 ## FURTHER READING

Freedman, S. G. (1990). *Small victories: The real world of a teacher, her students and their high school.* New York: Harper & Row.

Gitlin, A. (1992). *Teachers' voices for school change.* New York: College Teachers Press.

Heck, S. F., & Williams, C. R. (1984). *The complex roles of the teacher: An ecological perspective.* New York: Harper & Row.

Kidder, T. (1989). *Among schoolchildren.* Boston, MA: Houghton Mifflin.

Witherell, C., Noddings, N. (1992). *Stories lives tell: Narrative and dialogue in education.* New York: Teachers College Press.

Chapter Twenty

PARENTS AS PARTNERS

SETTING

Third Grade

FOCUS QUESTIONS

When reading this case, consider the following questions:

- How can you involve parents in their child's learning?
- How comfortable are you when talking to parents about your teaching and their child's learning?

J illian's nervousness was evident as she greeted me.

"Hi, Dr. McCollum," she said hesitantly. "Do you have a few minutes to talk?"

"Sure Jillian," I replied. "What's up?"

"Well, I'm really enjoying student teaching in Mrs. Stuart's third grade over at Northside Elementary," she went on, "but I think I've made some mistakes already, and I'm not sure what I can do to fix things."

Seeing that Jillian was on the verge of tears, I offered her a chair and sat down. "Tell me what the problem is," I urged.

"Well, I have a group of kids who range from nonreaders to some super bright kids. I have been using flexible groups to intermingle the kids based on what they know for various subjects and topics. I try to put the kids together who are having difficulty learning in some area for at least a part of the day. I also group together kids who are doing well sometimes. But I have one parent who is really upset with me and asked Mrs. Stuart to take over the 'higher end' group. Mrs. Stuart said that this parent didn't feel that I was meeting the needs of the talented kids."

"Is there a talented and gifted program in your setting?" I asked.

"The school uses a cluster model, where five to six kids from third grade to sixth grade are clustered in a classroom with a teacher who has been specifically trained to deal with these gifted kids. I know that I haven't had a lot of work with gifted education, but I think that I can provide enrichment opportunities for those kids. I had thought about giving them a chance to do literature circles, something that I was not prepared to do with the rest of the class, but this parent said that this was just abandoning the gifted kids and not providing them with any direct instruction. What should I do?"

"Have you talked with this parent yourself?" I asked.

"Oh no! Mrs. Stuart has been running interference for me. She is supportive of what I'm doing, but she said that this particular mom was very concerned about her child receiving appropriate instruction, and that this parent was not really supportive of the cluster model."

"What does the parent want?"

"I guess that she is most familiar with a program where gifted kids would be pulled out for separate instruction."

"How do you feel about that?"

"Well, I recognize that all children develop differently and have unique abilities and gifts, but I do think that a teacher can provide instruction that meets all of their needs."

"You might want to think about how you will develop the literature circles for this higher group and consider how you can convey this information to the parents of all of these children so they are reassured that instruction is appropriate," I suggested.

"Oh, I'm really nervous about talking to this parent," Jillian said.

"But Jillian, you will need to talk to the parents of all of your children and let them know how the kids are doing. This is an important part of being a teacher. If parents aren't informed, how can they be partners in their children's learning?"

"Well, I can do a good job of teaching, but I get confused when I have to explain myself to a parent," Jillian lamented.

"You won't be comfortable in developing a good working relationship with the parents unless you try it," I said. "Just think of it as a part of your practice teaching. You need to develop experience communicating with parents. Why don't you sit down and we'll write out a rationale for using literature circles as well as the rest of your curriculum, so that you can explain to this mom how you are providing for the needs of her child."

Jillian agreed, so we scheduled some time the next afternoon to meet with her cooperating teacher and draft a response to the concerned parent. The next day, our conversation with Mrs. Stuart provided some background. She said that the cluster program was new and that many parents were concerned that it might not be serving the bright kids as well as the lower-end students. "However," Mrs. Stuart went on, "I do believe that we need to give this model a chance. I think that the literature circles will give good readers a chance to develop their inferential reading ability by comparing and contrasting several books. Jillian's work expands on my plans—I was going to have that group read ahead in their text on their own, without the directed lesson that the rest of the class will receive. Jillian has brought in several other trade books with similar topics for the group to read and compare to the one in the text. Following our prereading activities, while the rest of the class is reading their story from the text, she is going to work with the advanced group. I think this is a wonderful extension of the original lesson."

"We were thinking about a project for the kids to do that would also be at a higher level of thinking," Jillian responded. "Although I believe that all of the kids in this room could do a project, we need to give them choices that fit their level a bit more."

Mrs. Stuart frowned. "For now, let's just give the gifted kids the project," she suggested.

With some hesitation, Jillian agreed. She wrote out her rationale and practiced calling the parent, using me in the other role. After several rehearsals, she said that she would talk to the parent that evening. The next day I called to ask how things had gone.

"Well, I was so nervous," Jillian began. "I actually used our script almost word for word so I wouldn't forget anything. She seemed okay with my plan, but said she would be anxious to see the books the students were reading and the list of projects. I was afraid she would yell at me, but she said that she was willing to withhold judgment until we finished the unit."

"That's good," I replied.

"Yes, but I have been thinking about the fact that only the parents of the really bright kids seem to get involved in the schools. Mrs. Stuart said that typically at conferences she sees only a few parents, and they are the ones who don't really need to come. I remember what we talked about in our methods class about using parents as partners. I think that I am going to generate a newsletter with some suggestions in it for parents to try with their kids at home. Maybe I can also keep them up to speed on what the class is doing and point out the extensions for the upper-end kids. Do you think that is a good idea?" Jillian asked.

"I think this is a wonderful way for you to connect with parents," I stated.

Several weeks later, I stopped to see how things were progressing in Jillian's room.

"Hi, Dr. McCollum!" Jill greeted me.

When I asked about her contact with parents, she shrugged. "I guess it is doing some good. I've been sending the newsletter out weekly and trying to point out what we are doing and including some student writing. I called a few parents whose kids were at the low end but who have been working really hard, and they seemed surprised that I would connect with positive news. Some of the children have told me that they did the little science experiment at home with the celery and food coloring that I suggested, so things are beginning to happen. I think I've given parents some ideas about how to reinforce at home what we do in school."

"Do you think that you have provided the gifted kids with enough options that stretch their thinking?"

"I'm not sure. I have tried to develop lessons that address the needs of a wide range of students. But, I don't really know what the parents' reaction is because I'm still nervous about talking with them."

"Why not call them and get their opinion about how they see things going?" I said. "You might ask them about their child's project, the newsletter, or describe the higher-order thinking that is going on as the students compare the books they read, just like you explained it to me."

"I don't know about that," Jillian replied. "What I want to do is to tell them that I know what I'm doing and that I can provide their child with an appropriate education. I get kind of defensive whenever I talk about this issue. I mean, I may be inexperienced, but I have almost completed my degree. These parents aren't teachers, so I'm not sure they really know about the methods I'm using. My student teaching will be over soon, so I think I'll just leave well enough alone."

⊚ POINTS TO PONDER

1. What are some other ideas for involving parents in their child's education?

2. How can you keep parents informed and updated regarding your teaching methods and curriculum?

3. How do you feel about talking with parents about your teaching philosophy and methods? How will you deal with angry or disgruntled parents?

4. How will you handle parent conferences? Do you plan to involve the child in the conference?

5. What are your plans for dealing with the wide range of abilities that are found in all classes at every grade level?

6. How can you determine the appropriate reading level for students so that class materials are not too easy or too difficult for the various students?

7. This student teacher is planning on waiting until she hears from parents who have had issues in the past. What are some possible outcomes of this approach? How might you contact parents in a way that is more comfortable for the teacher? Is contacting parents the responsibility of the student teacher, or should the cooperating teacher handle all of the parent calls and interactions?

✪ FURTHER READING

Berger, E. (1995). *Parents as partners in education: Families and schools working together.* Upper Saddle River, NJ: Merrill/Prentice Hall.

Comer, J. P. (1986). Parent participation in the schools. *Phi Delta Kappan, 67,* 442–466.

Greenwood, G., & Hickman, C. (1991). Research and practice in parent involvement: Implications for teacher education. *The Elementary School Journal, 91,* 279–288.

Henderson, A. (1988). Parents are a school's best friends. *Phi Delta Kappan, 70,* 148–153.

Morris, V., Taylor, S., Knight, J., & Wasson, R. (1996). Preparing Teachers to reach out to families and communities. *Action in Teacher Education, 18,* 10–22.

Pitton, D. (1996). Parent involvement in the schools: A new role for government and business. *New Schools, New Communities, 12:* 68–71.

Part Three

LOOKING BACK

*Experiences from the perspective
of one who has been there . . .*

Chapter Twenty-One

RETAKING STUDENT TEACHING: FAILURE OR FORTUNE?

SETTING

High School English

FOCUS QUESTIONS

When reading this case, consider the following questions:

- What are your fears about student teaching?
- What can you do to strengthen your skills so you can combat those fears?

SPRING SEMESTER—DAY 1

Well, today I officially became a student teacher. I felt uncomfortable coming into class today. I am sure that it's because right now I feel I don't belong. I am very glad I bothered to make a trip ahead of time to meet my cooperating teacher, Joyce, and get acquainted with the school.

It's been pretty much decided that I'll teach two sophomore English classes and one American Literature class. Since I had no designated place to go, I didn't see any point in arriving before my cooperating teacher's first class, which was second hour. I observed the second-hour class and all the other classes I'll have this semester. I also will accompany Joyce on lunch duty and hall duty throughout the day.

DAY 2

I observed again today. The students in the sophomore class are in a basic track, and it is evident in their behavior! Joyce is giving me a very brief unit to do on a short story for the sophomores. I think I will do the reading in class. I'd also like to do a response journal; they haven't done that yet this year. We talked about my assignment for American Lit. I will get two weeks to do *Of Mice and Men*. I'd better get cracking on a lesson plan. Also, she wants me to lead some discussion on *The Great Gatsby* by next week! Help!

DAY 3

I met with my college supervisor. I need to get some papers organized for her— keeping this journal is one of my assignments as well as jotting down some observational notes. I am glad to have someone from school to support me; I think I am going to need it. For some reason I feel less sure and less confident each passing day. I am getting most of the names of the sophomores down, but I don't know any of the American Lit. kids yet. I must read *Gatsby* and start plowing through some short stories this week to decide which one I will teach. I think that I am going to have to get at least one weekend day off from work at my 'paying' job.

DAY 4

Even though I've formulated some plans, I've yet to get them down on paper. That has got to be done. I corrected some essays for the sophomores, and I found it very hard. I am not sure how far these papers have to go to reflect the level the kids are capable of, but it seems a shame to put a final grade on these when there is much that could be done to improve them.

DAY 5

Joyce says Wednesday is the day I will lead the discussion on *Gatsby*. She has her lessons pretty well mapped out, I am taking notes all the time when we meet, but

I am not sure how I can create a lesson when she has everything so organized. Can these random notes of mine be turned into a lesson?

DAY 6

I got up in front of the class in American Lit. for the first time. I was amazed at how awkward and stilted I felt. I tried to lead a discussion on three chapters of *Gatsby*. It was apparent none of the kids had read the book. I finally ran out of discussion-generating questions and told them to read for the rest of the period. They need to catch up. I have to plan my lessons for *Of Mice and Men* carefully because Joyce wants me to stay with the other class that she has during last period, so we complete the unit at the same time.

DAY 8

I had the hour in American Lit. to do an opinion worksheet and talk about the American Dream. I managed to keep going for 35 to 40 minutes. My small groups got out of hand. I had trouble controlling the talking after the groups broke up. I think they were challenging me.

I've got the short story unit pretty well mapped out. That starts Wednesday. I've gotten the stories copied and I need to write a list of questions for the final. Haven't had that "good" day yet—I am still waiting. I haven't had a class that's "mine" yet.

DAY 9

I had good feedback on small groups in their responses to questions on *Of Mice and Men*. They were to find a paragraph that might indicate theme and find two examples of foreshadowing. We found five!

The short story unit was awful during fourth hour. The kids just didn't respond. I quickly revamped my approach for the next hour. Fifth hour did seem to go better. (Mostly though, I think it was just that I was more prepared, having had one class to try things out.) I can see how experience really helps. Now that I've tried the story "The Tiger or the Lady," I would use the same material, but I would know HOW to use it more effectively!

DAY 10

I am getting pages of feedback from Joyce. They're very helpful as she points out all of the things I need to do better. However, they seem to be shifting my focus. I find myself trying to please her rather than dealing directly with class. I got great response from the task of writing an ending to "The Tiger or the Lady." The kids did a nice job. I read their papers aloud, and they all wanted me to read theirs.

DAY 11

Gatsby discussions in American Lit. were pretty lousy. I had to carry the class. Most (maybe even all) of the kids had not read the daily assignments. They truly bombed the first quiz. I don't think that it works to cover a heavy duty novel like *Death of a Salesman* in class and require something as difficult as *The Great Gatsby* to be done as homework at the same time! Joyce has such a wealth of knowledge that she often changes plans right before class. This works after all of her years of experience, but when she makes last-minute suggestions for change, I feel panicky!

DAY 12

Boy, the sophomores are hard to figure out. I think they're bored and inattentive when I am reading a story; then they answer questions pretty well or write in their journals that they really liked the story. The journal idea is working well. It gives me some one-on-one feedback, and I need that from each student. I've found that with every story, some kids absolutely hate it, yet some kids love it. I must have had enough variety in the selections we read because I heard different responses from different kids each time. One student turned in a super "new" ending to the story "August Heat." It was incredibly well written—and from a kid in a basic class. I also am hearing some very thoughtful answers; they often hit the nail on the head so accurately in our discussions.

DAY 13

I am not so sure about how things are going with Joyce. She's really giving me a lot of input, but I feel I am being watched like a hawk. I've got to work on ignoring her. My sense is that it would be difficult to talk to her about my feelings. When I've come close to the subject, she emphasizes the fact that the class is ultimately her concern. If I don't whip them into shape, she says she'll have to contend with it when I leave. She says she wants to give me *carte blanche* on lesson plans and daily stuff, as long as I stay within her overall plans. It's very hard. While I know I can do that and I'm willing to put the work into it, I still have to focus on *her* idea of discipline and control. I tend to allow the students a little rope and then tug when my parameters have been reached. I don't feel I can be myself in situations where Joyce expects such complete control. I need a comfort level and warmth to function well, and I do not get that feeling from this classroom.

DAY 14

I think that I know one of the secrets to the discipline question. This week in both the basic sophomore and American Lit. classes I got angry. When that happened, I knew, and the kids knew, that they had pushed too far. It was amazing how effective sincerity was. I really believed that they had violated the basic rules of the classroom and of respect for others. I wasn't playing teacher or dictator—I was relating to the class on a real level. My honest and heartfelt comments about their behavior seemed to set the boundaries a little more clearly. I think that when I begin a class of my own and establish my own atmosphere and class rules, things will go more smoothly. I am tempted to ask if I can have the first day of the next semester alone—in both classes. I am certainly glad that my college student teaching time-frame allows for me to complete this semester and begin the next at this school. I really think it will be valuable to see both the ending of a term and to begin a relationship with the students in the following semester.

DAY 15

My comfort level is a little better— but not much. I still get a knot in my stomach just before every class. Fortunately, I am told, my nervousness doesn't show.

Joyce seems even more reluctant to let me design my own curriculum or even select readings for American Lit. that don't coincide with her plans. She has a final exam that she has no desire to change. (I even offered to write a new one!) It is disappointing because I've been coming up with some great ideas. I've learned, very quickly, that I am limited here because of the inflexibility of my cooperating teacher and the lack of availability of materials.

DAY 22

I haven't been able to write in this journal for awhile. I am finding this experience more stressful than I realized. I am getting more anxious about getting in front of the class each day instead of less anxious. I like working with the kids one on one or putting them in small groups and facilitating the learning, but standing in front of 30 to 35 kids is really hard. Lesson plans are difficult too. I think I am being too particular; I plan and then reject a lot of ideas and continually start over. I want to impress Joyce, be original, and really engage the kids, but nothing seems good enough.

DAY 23

I am putting more time and effort into my teaching every day. I haven't done one other thing except work on daily plans. I work all week-nights and all day Sunday on my plans. I've had to stop working at my other job on Saturdays because I am always doing something for school. I have no social life, because I am consumed with generating lessons that will please Joyce. She always finds something that isn't right though.

DAY 24

Yesterday was interesting. We had a large-group seminar back at college, and I compared notes with quite a few of the other student teachers. Their experiences are all different, but none are quite like mine. No one feels that they are under such close scrutiny as I am. I feel that I am being picked apart piece by piece. No one is getting as much negative feedback as I am. I must either be doing an extremely poor job or have found myself in a very unique situation. Since I think student teaching is a time of learning and a time for making mistakes, I expected some criticism, but that's all I get—and I get it daily. I find it immobilizing. I am becoming more and more self-conscious. I feel stilted and artificial in front of the class. Shouldn't I be better than I was the first day?

DAY 25

This semester I have to travel from one room for the sophomore basic English class down the hall to another room for American Lit. and then back to the first room for the second sophomore class, and this is tough. So far I've been able to pull together all my materials for each class, but I am waiting for the day that I forget something. I rush into class and try to be smooth and relaxed the moment the bell rings, but taking roll and quieting the kids is a weak point that I have to keep working on. I arrive to class breathless, because it seems that many kids want or need to talk with me after class, and I need to head off down the hall. I suppose it is good to have all my classes in a row, but I wish I had my hall duty supervision between so I could think for a few minutes!

DAY 33

I haven't gotten any positive feedback for awhile. My college supervisor observed me and liked the class. She asked me about the decisions I had made for the lesson and seemed pleased that I had developed some of my own materials. Joyce rejected my idea of a talk about prejudice today. I have some handouts on the Ku Klux Klan and their use of public television and some Jesse Helms material from newspapers and magazines. She feels that the basic tenth graders need to stick to the text. She has taught this novel many times.

I really wanted to read Zora Neale Hurston's "How It Feels to Be Colored Me"—again, Joyce wasn't enthused. She says there isn't time if we want to cover the text. I worked hours on a Jeopardy game using trivia from the book. We didn't use it. Joyce doesn't like to have the kids too excited or loud. She says there needs to be a purpose in each thing we do. I thought a review that was fun might get these kids to recognize what they know about this book. Couldn't the purpose of a review game demonstrate that reading literature can be fun?

DAY 35

Today my college supervisor told me that Joyce thought it would be best if I were not to continue my work in her classroom. She cited that my lack of attention to detail (especially in regard to record keeping and attendance), my loose classroom management style, and my unconnected lesson plans were the reason for this. I am supposed to complete my student teaching in another placement this fall. In the meantime, I have been advised to think about how I might improve in these areas.

I am totally ashamed and defeated. . . . I am not sure that I will go through this again next fall.

FALL SEMESTER—DAY 10

After two weeks—one a preparation week where we all worked to get ready for the first day of school—I feel I need to take time to think about what's happened. First, have I enjoyed the past nine days? I'd have to answer a resounding "YES!" Second, do I feel I've accomplished anything? A resounding "I'm not sure." So far all is running quite smoothly, and my new cooperating teacher, Susan, is helping to iron out the kinks and is sharing her experience in working out the details. That, as it always has been, is still my biggest problem: the little details. The techniques of modeling, small groups, and discussion are things I wanted to use, but in what order and exactly in what way? Susan's help was life-saving. I worry a lot about what the week would have been like without her.

During this summer, I did a lot of thinking about my previous student teaching experience. It is easy to look back and see where I made mistakes. I took a personality test at the college and was reminded that I am a random thinker. My previous cooperative teacher had definitely been more concrete, and because my ideas were more divergent, I probably seemed to be disjointed and unorganized. I thought about trying to change and become more linear in my approach to the classroom, but it seemed to me that this personality shift might be impossible. Still, I know that I have to make lists and plans that establish a perspective and provide a focus for the students because they need to know where we are going with a lesson and why we are learning something. I know that I can do that; still, I don't want to teach if I cannot be myself. I had many teachers who were creative and abstract, and I liked that. Many of my students may also be more abstract thinkers, but I guess what I have to do is be structured enough to help those who also need more organization in the classroom.

Things that stick out in my mind from these past few weeks include Susan's comment that chaos could result if you don't think out the little things ahead of time. I know that this is a challenge for me, but how do I focus on these little things when I want to jump ahead to the big picture? I can decide to use small groups for a discussion—that's easy. What I forget to do is think about how I am going to divide the class into groups. Susan pointed out that this isn't something to agonize over either, but that you do have to have a plan. For this grouping issue, I suggested the method of having students count off, but it seemed so boring and old hat. I wanted something new and different. Then I came up with the idea of giving them a number when they came in the room, but decided that they'd figure out the system and exchange numbers to be with their friends. This planning could go on and on, I told Susan, but she just smiled. She said that any of the choices I mentioned would work, and that I should try not to spend too much time with the little decisions.

I now see that I need to lay out my lesson plan in much more detail. Why wasn't that mentioned to me before? It seems so clear now! On the other hand, I can't sweat the small stuff. Whenever I feel that I am losing control and running around like a chicken with its head cut off, I have noticed that this is when I am going round and round and not committing to a plan. In retrospect, I am spending too much time on the little stuff. Since this is the hardest part for me, I have little confidence in my decisions, so I want to figure out each angle. Susan mentioned that perhaps I should start with the end point, where I want the lesson to go, and work backwards. This was a great idea! This seems to help me get things organized, and by starting with the big picture, I can determine the overall goals and then determine the details that need to be in place without putting all my time into the small decisions.

I feel more prepared for student teaching this time, and I am beginning to feel more excited than nervous! I have two American Literature classes and two writing classes to deal with. I will be here for eight weeks of classes (nine weeks counting the week of preparation). I still worry about whether I will make it this time. I couldn't handle another failure. It took several conversations with my college professors this summer, and lots of time thinking about my personal approach to teaching, to get me to face a classroom again. I worry that I might find myself slipping into old patterns of disorganization like last semester. I worry about my students. They need something from this class. It's not fair for them to spend one hour of their precious time without getting something in return. So far, the kids have been pretty good, and I think they've gotten a good feel for what's going to happen in the classes I am assigned to. It is so helpful that Susan is talking TO me (not AT me) and showing me how she makes decisions. She is a wonderful role model. I feel like I might be able to do this.

DAY 11

I have been noticing the characteristics of my classes—they vary so much. In American Lit. I feel that third hour just isn't as cooperative. They're fighting most of what we do. One group of guys seem to hate this class (and English in general). Susan and I are working to create a more comfortable atmosphere to help offset their attitude. We did some socialization activities today. This really helps me. I have discovered that I am much more comfortable when I work on a more personal level with the students. I am getting to know them as people, and this helps me make decisions about lessons. I like that Susan and I introduced ourselves and shared some of "who we are" with the class. This way, they seem to be opening up to us. I think that I will follow Susan's example and always try to build a sense of community among my classes at the beginning of each semester.

DAY 12

I want to do more of this journal keeping, but I have trouble finding time for this activity. I am going to record bits and pieces because some things are happening that I need to get down.

One of the students brought me a book that he wants me to read. I'm flattered. He was interested in the fact that I took a course in Japanese Literature. He asked some questions, so I gave him a book by Mishima called *The Man Who Fell from Grace with the Sea,* and he read it in two days! I've looking for some other authors that will keep him interested. The book he gave me is called *Ninja*—it doesn't look like it's "up my alley," but I am going to read it so we can discuss it.

Susan and I developed the syllabus with input from the students and a leading list of objectives from us. I had suggested this to Susan the first day we met, as I had felt that part of my problem last year was that I was trying to teach what someone else had planned. Susan had responded that she usually generated a syllabus for the students and offered to let me create the part I was to teach. There were so many options that I couldn't decide what to teach, and when I suggested to Susan that maybe we ought to let the students decide what they wanted to focus on, she seemed eager to try it out. The thought of preparing a whole syllabus had been scary to me, but with all of us working together, I think we came up with a very interesting and intense course. Today we are printing copies of the final draft of this class plan. The students still seem wary, unsure of what to make of this idea of our writing the syllabus together. They had some questions and were not very responsive to my initial rough draft, but both Susan and I think it's because they are used to being told what they will study rather than being asked. There is so much literature that can be incorporated into a study of American literature that it was easy to provide a list of options and let them select what they wanted to focus on as a class. I think they will feel a sense of ownership when they get their copy today. It was a great exercise in the process of writing and a great way to start the class. We shared and combined ideas and proofread and edited together from the ideas and rough drafts I put together. I now have 16 strong objectives that the class voted to pursue. This semester I shouldn't hear "Why are we studying or doing this?" because we hashed all of that out as we put the syllabus together!

DAY 13

The chemistry or personality of my classes still varies a great deal. The third-hour American Lit. class didn't do much with their journal responses—I gave them four choices! They just didn't write very much. Most of them rewrote the essay we had read into a poem; this was the option that required the least effort. No one responded well to the performances (the readings) of their classmates. I thought the problem might be that kids were too far away from the speaker and couldn't hear or see what they had written on the board. I am reorganizing the room so we don't have such long rows (it was four rows of eight seats). Now we have five rows of six or seven seats, which will get more kids up front and close to the action. I like bring closer to everyone; it makes the class more active. Susan also enjoys lively discussions. She has never commented on the class being out of control. Her observations to me are more about how I can guide the class more effectively with the kinds of questions I ask. Fifth-hour American Lit. class wrote some terrific responses to the assignment—good, detailed essays. The two classes are like night and day.

DAY 14

My writing classes are settling in. Some students have dropped from the class—I tend to take that personally, as if I failed to entice the students to stay. Some students have commented that there is a lot of homework. We've been giving it out a week or so ahead of time. If the kids write it down and pace themselves, it shouldn't be too difficult to do it all. They need to get used to this, having to plan their own homework loads and schedule what they need to accomplish will be vital in college or in any job, for that matter. They still want me to tell them each night what is due tomorrow instead of checking their assignment lists. I think that part of the purpose of this class is to prepare them to handle being independent learners, so I am making them work this through themselves.

I worry a little about our Swedish exchange student. He's been lonely; he commented in a journal response that there are hours during the day when he is miserable. I've talked to one group (about half of the class) about the school's reputation for cliques. They all agree but never do anything about it. Can I foster a sense of inclusiveness in my classes so we can combat the cliques?

I think the writing kids are eager for some creative activities. We will hopefully be ready to move into that area tomorrow. Susan is letting me try an exercise I created in writing descriptions of people—we'll see how it goes.

I am really enjoying the students. I like talking to them one on one. But I worry about a few in each of the American Lit. classes. They obviously have problems reading and have to go slowly. I'd like to help. I think that I'll mention that they should come and talk to me if they feel they are having trouble keeping up. Maybe I could read to them? Maybe I could put some of the chapters on tape for them to listen to so they can catch up? I'll check with Susan on this.

DAY 15

I checked journals today. Most of them have a good start and are trying to keep up. I don't want to lose these kids. They all seemed to like discussing the book and having reading time in class. I think it is important to respect their wishes and give them SOME of what they want. It is their class. Susan seems to be on the same wavelength as I am regarding student needs.

Two girls in seventh-hour writing class wrote a couple of terrific essays. I loved listening to what they came up with. Some really surprised me. Susan is great! My comfort level continues to increase. It is refreshing to feel like a colleague instead of someone who is not up to par. I actually look forward to leading a lesson. What really helps me and works for me is to talk a little with the students when they come in. If I can get into a conversation with one or two, I feel relaxed and it leads into starting class in a more comfortable manner. I guess some teachers would say that I don't have a clear beginning to the class, but we ease into the learning and I can often connect what we are talking about to what we are doing in class—that just feels so natural. I don't feel as if I'm going "on stage" every hour. I realize now that I was looking at teaching as if it was a performance and therefore was literally getting stage-fright. Also, I don't work well with that imaginary wall between the students and myself. I like the connectedness that Susan and I have created among our students and ourselves.

DAY 20

Last week was full, busy, and rewarding. I haven't found time to put my thoughts down into this journal until today! The highlight of the week for me was sixth-hour writing class. My new college supervisor observed earlier in the day (fourth-hour American Lit.), and she seemed to enjoy what we were doing and had several compliments for me after class! I think that the whole unit has ended up working very well. The final discussion on Monday was productive because of the preliminary work done in the small groups.

I thought the American Lit. classes all went very well, but the writing class during sixth hour was a joy. I am now working totally on my own in there, and I already know that I am going to miss it when the quarter is over. The class is a model of the value of diversity. We have an exchange student from Sweden who has been a delight, full of ideas that he's more than willing to express about our culture. I had brought an article entitled "We Have Reason to Believe We Think Too Much," which proposed that we do not use our natural skills of intuition and instinct and that we rationalize too much—actually to the point of making harm-ful or incorrect decisions. It was a real criticism of Western thought. Somehow from this we got into an hour-long discussion with everyone interested and par-ticipating about an entire range of subjects, including reincarnation. One student (another delight) is Indian and a Hindu. She held the kids spellbound as she talked about the levels of life experiences the Hindu believe they must go through to reach the final place, or highest level of immortality. Some may say we were off the subject, but I made sure I pointed out that good writing can inspire creative and critical thinking. It was rewarding to watch the students become so interested and involved. Many were able to generate ideas for a writing topic that day, which was our objective, and they all seemed excited about communicating their thoughts through their writing.

DAY 22

I have spent a lot of time talking with Eric, our exchange student. He seems so lonely and homesick at times. He is such a well-educated person; he's been all over the world. I think he intimidated the other kids at first because he speaks and reads several languages and knows so much more about art and literature than our kids. But he is warming up in class discussions and can be very funny. I've suggested to a couple of the kids who are leaders and involved in activities such as homecoming that they should try to make sure he is included in the activities. I am going to have him over for supper soon with my husband and me. He's told me he is hungry for boiled vegetables and is tired of the fat in our diets. I think it was a hint.

DAY 23

My other favorite class is fourth-hour America Lit. I really like this group of kids. At first I wondered if they might think they could wrap me around their little fingers, so to speak, but it doesn't work that way. That class tries very hard to do well for me, and they worry a little about disappointing me—which is neat. They asked if they were doing okay after my last observation by my college supervisor. I have told how impressed I am when their work is good. It is amazing what a little encouragement will do.

I think the students liked the novel, *Staggerford*, in general. I worry about making sure they get enough from me to assist in their understanding. I don't want them to ever be shortchanged by my inexperience. Susan is a big help with this. We talk every morning, and the things she points out help me see and remember to pay attention to the details of the lesson.

DAY 24

Second-hour writing class got very upset this week. Thomas, who has been (and I think over all, is) generally quite cooperative, started right in letting us have it on Wednesday. First of all, he came about a minute late—again. He comes from the other side of the school and usually slips in after the bell. Anyway, he was angry about that and said that he hated the rules that the school enforced, including everybody's having to be someplace exactly to the minute. I have felt that he, and many others, try to pack too many activities into their lives. He plays football and has a heavy class load. The stress came to a head that day, and he took it out on us. I don't think he is getting his paper done. He chose to criticize our class and the lack of structure. We do spend a lot of time writing, rewriting, editing, and discussing writing style. He got a couple of other kids behind him, and they all had questions about assignments.

What it boiled down to was that they can't handle getting assignments several weeks ahead of time, and they don't like not being given specific topics for their papers. This approach is really new for them. I didn't realize they would be so used to structure. At first I felt bad and thought that maybe my approach was poor and that this was a dumb idea. But then I realized that it was just more reason to argue that they need this. These kids have no idea what college will be like. The whole purpose of this elective writing class is to prepare them for college writing. We talked a little about that, and I gave them my perspective of college and the need to be self-disciplined. We offered some more ownership in the class and invited dialogue with the kids. I asked them to bring their suggestions and was surprised at the comments the next day. Thomas, who initiated the discussion, said that he really liked the class. He had blown off steam and seemed ready to be realistic about what was expected of him. He added that the approach Susan and I were taking was different and that he was getting more than just writing skills from the class.

Several of the students shared their assignment and daily calendars with the other students and offered suggestions for time management. Both are essential tools for good students and are really necessary for survival in college. One girl was giving the boys sticky notes to put on the front of the textbooks to show how she writes her assignments right on the book. I guess I should have expected some fallout with this self-directed approach. I told the students that it was like falling down when you were learning to ski or ice skate—you don't fall unless you are stretching yourself and trying new things.

DAY 26

I have noticed a strong gender-specific response in my writing classes. I've realized that the four or five students who are having trouble with the open assignments and the forum in writing are all male. Contrast this to the fact that one third of the students in both classes are getting good solid A's, and they are all girls. The boys who seem to be having trouble want us to assign specific topics, a specific type of essay, and a specific number of pages for each assignment. They can't handle the free-writing and open discussion that we have been using to generate ideas for topics. I guess they're all concrete and sequential in their approach to learning. The way I see it, they are the students who will probably benefit most from the class, as it is forcing them to take ownership for their learning. Still, I might offer a few specific options for some of the assignments to help them feel more comfortable and successful. I will want to explain WHY I am offering some specific choices, though, or I might undermine the positive effects that have come from this approach.

DAY 28

We have been reading *Dances with Wolves* in American Lit., and it has been so much fun! There is so much to work with in this novel. The Native American culture is interesting to all of the kids in the class. I have only one so far who has written negative, prejudicial statements in his journal responses. I have a feeling that it stems from the spear-fishing debate, as he has written about his love of hunting and fishing. He didn't state an issue specifically, but he talked about Native Americans wanting special privileges. I'd like to think he'll gain a little insight into this issue from our studies.

I did a mini-lecture on wolves. One of the journal questions or assignments was to write an essay or poem about why the wolf Two Socks was alone on the prairie. The students really got into it. My brief talk was lengthened because of all of their questions. We seem to be bringing more kids into the discussion and enjoyment of the literature by focusing on a variety of topics related to the novel. Every day somebody brings something to show us. They bring pictures of their

Husky dogs, native jewelry, and magazine articles. They are really making a connection between what we read and their lives. I love it! I sent them to the art store to look at and report on some Native American art that I had seen exhibited. They liked that too! It surprised me to see which kids got caught up in discussing the art. Many boys who said they had never been to an art store or been interested in art really enjoyed this task and said they would even like to own some of this art!

DAY 30

A highlight from our "Wolves" unit: Susan lead the class in a Native American chant one sunny afternoon. Of course the kids said they felt sort of silly, but they went along with us anyway and seemed to enjoy it. They said they felt the power that the main character must have felt as he danced around the fire chanting one night.

Some students have asked me about my views about college and careers. These chats in the halls and before class seem to create more connections, but I am careful not to play counselor or take time away from our lessons.

Ten days left of my assignment here. I believe that I am being a responsible teacher, and I am treated as a peer by Susan and many of the other faculty members. What a wonderful feeling! I realize that I see my students as individuals. Last spring I was focusing on the entire class and keeping them under control and on task. Susan has pointed out that my more personal style works well when I view classes as a collection of individuals. I have totaled up the points from all of the work students have completed in my classes, and they look reasonable. On a percentage basis, I've got a good representation of A's, B's, and C's. If they're doing the work, they are awarded points and their grade reflects it. A couple of kids have not completed many assignments in my sixth-hour writing class. I hate to lead them by the hand, but I did give them some help the last few days as well as a chance to do some makeup work. My goal is to help them be successful writers, and they have to complete some work. The more specific guidelines seemed to help. Now, it's up to them to see if they can meet the challenge or not.

DAY 39

The last two weeks have flown by. My college supervisor and Susan conferred with me earlier this week, and both were very complimentary. In particular, they said I have the ability to connect with students and involve them in their learning. I have to say that Susan let me teach the way that fit with my philosophy and personality, yet she also helped me shape the loose ends of my lessons. She modeled her planning process and helped me organize and write good questions so that my discussions were focused. Susan provided me with the opportunity to try things my way, and she didn't worry about getting the class back under control after I left. She made me feel like a partner in the teaching and let me build my confidence until I could go solo. I had my self-confidence shattered last fall, but I realize that I just needed to work in another environment to develop my skills. If

I hadn't needed to extend my student teaching, I would never have met Susan, and my teaching skills would still be limited. I want to always remain open to learning and growing as a teacher. I am utterly amazed sometimes that my failure provided me with the good fortune of working with a skilled mentor who enabled me to become a strong, confident beginning teacher.

POINTS TO PONDER

1. Does your college have a system for enabling you to withdraw from a student teaching experience that you do not feel is supportive or in which you do not feel you will succeed?

2. Legally, what is the responsibility of the school you are placed in when there are serious questions about your performance? What are the responsibilities of your college or department of education?

3. Could you create a positive experience out of a seeming failure in student teaching?

4. How important is it for you to have a supportive cooperating teacher?

5. How will you deal with negative comments or criticism that might be given to you following an observation?

6. How might your personality, your own learning style, and your teaching philosophy affect the way you will engage students in your future classroom?

7. What perception might others have of you as a result of your personality, learning style, or philosophy that might be problematic in your work as a teacher?

FURTHER READING

Borich, G. (1993). *Clearly outstanding.* Needham Heights, MA: Allyn & Bacon.

Doyle, W. (1986). Classroom organization and management. In Whittrock, M. (Ed.), *Handbook of research on teaching.* New York: Macmillan.

Friebus, R. (1977). Agents of socialization involved in student teaching. *Journal of Educational Research, 70,* 263–268.

Pitton, D. (1994, September). Mentoring: The special needs of student teachers. *People and Education, 2,* 338–352.

Schubert, W., & Ayers, W. (Ed.). (1992). *Teacher lore: Learning from our own experience.* White Plains, NY: Longman.

Chapter Twenty-Two

THE WAY IT WAS

SETTING

Sixth-Grade Teacher (15-Year Veteran)

FOCUS QUESTIONS

When reading this case, consider the following questions:

- Where do you see yourself in 15 years?
- How might your student teaching affect the direction that your career takes in the future?

This past semester I had a student teacher in my sixth-grade classroom, and it really made me stop and think about my own beginning experience 15 years ago. At that time, I knew that I wanted to teach, but I really didn't see the connection between what we did in my education classes and what was going on in my student teaching placement. I was very confident, and perhaps my years of experience as a camp counselor and swimming instructor had given me the experiential learning that enabled me to make it through student teaching. Either that, or I was very lucky. I really did not have much support or encouragement from my cooperating teacher. Because of my own past experiences, and because of my current belief that working with student teachers allows educators to help shape the future of our profession, I really take my role as a cooperating teacher seriously. I devise a plan for interacting with my student teacher based on what I do not want to occur—that is, a repetition of my own student teaching experience.

I chose to student teach by location. I think student teachers today ought to be placed in a setting where they will be supported, but I wanted to be able to carpool to this school. I knew several other students from my college would be working at this site—and they had cars. I later found out that my placement was made by the principal, who asked for volunteers. It seems that Don Lionel usually offered to take a student teacher every spring. He was a coach for the junior high, and he said that he appreciated the extra help second semester, during basketball season. I was assigned to his sixth grade. I have taught a number of other grades since then, but I really do like the older kids, and find myself, in a sense, back where I started.

I didn't have a bad student teaching experience. I just didn't learn a lot. I used the time to do what I knew I could do well rather than focus on what I needed to improve. I had to find out when I got into my first full-time position the following year that I really didn't organize my classroom very efficiently. No one had pointed this out to me during student teaching, although the piles of materials that I left in corners of Don's room ought to have given him a clue that I might be a bit disorganized. How could I possibly be expected to keep track of attendance, lunch money, and field trip information, let alone all of the student work that I faced over the whole school year? I had no clue how to handle it all, and during the short time I student taught, it seemed more manageable. There was an end in sight, and if I left a mess, the consequences of this never caught up with me. I could keep everything together for 10 weeks, and even when I couldn't always find my daily lesson plan, Don never knew. I was never given any suggestions, nor did I received any negative comments. When I finished student teaching, I had a false sense of my own abilities. I was unprepared for the intensity of the ongoing, day-to-day routines and planning that are part of the rhythm of the school year.

Don winged his teaching quite a bit. He had been teaching sixth grade for over 10 years, and I suppose that he did have a lot of his lessons committed to memory. I needed to write out everything, and I would have benefited from some feedback on my lessons. Instead, I used notes that I scribbled on legal pads that nobody looked at. My college supervisor came out one time, and I had the students doing a performance, so of course, I didn't have a lesson plan to show him. No one asked me what I was thinking, no one asked me if I liked what I was doing, and no one told me what I did well or offered suggestions when the lessons flopped. I was on my own.

I liked the freedom of having my own class. After the first week, when Don saw that I could handle myself reasonably well in the classroom, he retreated to the faculty lounge to work on game plans for his basketball team. This didn't bother me at all. I had been creating programming for campers and getting water-phobic swimmers into the water for years. I knew that I was doing okay, and I liked that nobody questioned my work. It seemed like an affirmation of my skills. However, the question I have now, is how much better could I have been, and how much better would I be NOW, if I had had some direction during that first, formative teaching experience.

I remember that my student teaching class was reading biographies of presidents, so I thought I'd have them do a play about George Washington. This seemed to me to be a great way to get the kids involved with what they were reading. I searched for a simple drama and assigned parts to as many of the kids as I could. What I hadn't expected was that some students wouldn't want to perform in front of their friends. Of course, I made the ones I had selected perform, and I ignored the pleas of the others. After all, there were more parts for boys than girls, so obviously more ladies were "backstage." The time that I took with rehearsals really cut into our math and science time. No one asked me about these other subjects. I preferred language arts anyway, as it was more fun to teach what I liked. The play went over fairly well, I was able to get most of the kids to say their lines loud enough to be heard, and those who had fussed too much about performing had been put in charge of costumes. The cotton wigs and paper hats were not very elaborate, but I felt that this task had at least kept everyone busy. My college supervisor, on hand for the show, had been excited about my willingness to involve the children in the learning. I had just thought it would be more fun than reading all of the time.

I really wanted the kids to have fun while they were learning, so I made up some games, like Jeopardy, to review for tests. This seemed to me, however, to be counter to what serious teachers did, so I kept the fun stuff at a minimum. I still had my ability groups for reading and math, and I kept the others busy with worksheets while I pulled kids out to do fractions at the board or plow through their basal readers. Some of the material in the texts seemed boring, but I knew that I had to get the kids ready to pass their tests. I prided myself on the tests that I created. Some were very hard, and certainly only those students who really knew their stuff would get an A. I used my college text to help me devise good questions, and I thought that a multiple-choice test was the best way to assess all subjects. Sometimes I wrote funny options on test items, but I didn't show anyone these questions; I didn't want to appear frivolous or silly in my work.

When I think back to my student teaching, I see that my curriculum was very loosely structured and my students were taught as I had been taught. I never was given a curriculum guide to help me focus my teaching. Even though I liked a more active classroom, I knew the rules: Keep them quiet and in their seats. I had no one to talk to about my questions, and I wanted to make a good impression, so I shut the door to my classroom and did the best I could. I got wonderful evaluations from my cooperating teacher, who reappeared on occasion and told me what a fabulous job I was doing, as well as from my college supervisor, who loved the show I put on. No one challenged me to explain how my practice connected with educational theory, no one questioned my rationale or asked me "Why are you doing that?" As a result, I never really thought about teaching, I just did it.

When I got my first job the following fall, I kept doing what I had been doing the previous spring. My lack of organization, however, caught up with me over time. I lost important forms that had to be turned in, and the administration got mad. I let my kids shout out answers during our game reviews, and other teachers got upset and asked me to keep my class quiet. Parents complained when I took time from math to devote to dramatizations of our reading text. Suddenly, everything that I had been doing right during student teaching seemed to be wrong.

I guess you could say that I "toughed it out." I bought myself another file cabinet and kept my desk more organized. I wrote out schedules for the day so that I didn't run out of time to teach any subject. I made brightly colored cards for the kids to hold up during quiz games so they didn't have to shout. I survived, and I managed to become a pretty effective teacher. When I began work on my masters degree, my education classes seemed to be more focused on methodology, and I discovered cooperative learning and began using more student involvement in my teaching. I now know why I want children to have a real-life engagement with their reading, and I now use a whole language approach and real books. We cut up pizza when we work with fractions, and my tests now ask the children to explain *how* they know something is right or *why* something happened.

When I look back, I wonder how much more I might have learned if someone had asked me about my teaching during student teaching. Perhaps it wouldn't have been so hard to make the changes, and I might have had a less stressful first year of teaching. I am amazed that I stuck with teaching those first few years. With no one to talk to or share my ideas, it was a wonder I didn't quit!

Today I work on a team of sixth-grade teachers, and we plan together for all of our lessons. These changes have come slowly, but I am more committed to student learning, and not just concerned about what I want to do in the classroom. Our team works to connect the subjects across disciplines, and active learning is a primary method of teaching. When I have a student teacher, I really stay connected. They may be a little annoyed that I ask to see their lessons and make suggestions, but I want them to observe and try multiple approaches that support student learning. I wish that I hadn't had to figure all of this out on my own!

It is hard to believe sometimes that I have been in education for 15 years, but I really enjoy teaching. I want my student teachers to be sure that this life—the constant planning, the creative and reflective processes, the dedication to ensuring that all kids learn—is part of what they see in their future. I don't want them to have a false sense of what teaching is all about. I also want them to be comfortable interacting with their colleagues. I thought I had to do it all alone; I didn't realize for a long time the value of teaming with other teachers. Our conversations about teaching and effective practice are helpful to me as well—I get to hear about new innovations, discuss my philosophy, and see other ideas for helping students learn. Student teachers coming out of college today will need to be accountable for all of the teaching tasks, and so realistically, they need to practice handling it all. However, I am not about to just walk out the door and let them figure it all out on their own. By modeling, conferencing, team-teaching, and offering support and empathy, I hope that I can help these future teachers start their careers with a realistic vision of their future as educators. I just hope that the future teachers who work with me will be willing to accept my direction and guidance.

POINTS TO PONDER

1. What have you learned about yourself during your preservice teaching courses? Do you know how you learn and study most effectively? What are your favorite subjects? How can knowledge about yourself and your learning style affect your teaching? How will this information affect the way you teach?

2. This teacher spoke of the learning that took place after her student teaching. Discuss ways you plan to continue to develop your teaching after you get your teacher's license.

3. Do you know what strengths you bring to the classroom? Do you know the areas in which you need to continue to improve?

4. Discuss how you can use your student teaching as an opportunity to practice and hone all of the skills needed by teachers in the classroom.

5. How can you be proactive in preparing for student teaching so that you will maximize this learning experience?

6. Consider your long-range plans. Where do you see yourself in 15 years, and how will you prepare yourself to get there?

FURTHER READING

Bogue, E. G. (1991). *A journey of the heart: The call to teaching.* Bloomington, IN: Phi Delta Kappa Educational Foundation.

Gehrke, N. (1987). *On being a teacher.* West Lafayette, IN: Kappa Delta Pi.

Gosnell, J. (1977). The relationship between work experience and occupational aspirations and attrition from teaching. *The Clearinghouse, 51,* 176–179.

Lieberman, A., & Miller, L. (1984). *Teachers, their world and their work.* Alexandria, VA: Association for Supervision and Curriculum Development.

Murnane, R. J., & Phillips, B. R. (1981). Learning by doing, vintage and selection: Three pieces of the puzzle relating teaching experience and teaching performance. *Economics of Education Review, 1*(4), 453–466.

Sarason, S. (1993). *You are thinking of teaching?* San Francisco, CA: Jossey-Bass Publishers.

Index